P9-DNE-376

Moses and Monotheism

Sigmund Freud

Moses and Monotheism

Translated from
the German
by Katherine Jones

VINTAGE BOOKS

A DIVISION OF RANDOM HOUSE

New York

VINTAGE BOOKS
are published by Alfred A. Knopf, Inc.
and Random House, Inc.

Copyright 1939 by Sigmund Freud. All rights reserved
under International and Pan-American Copyright Conventions.
Copyright renewed 1967 by Ernst L. Freud.

Manufactured in the United States of America

VINTAGE BOOKS
are published by ALFRED A. KNOPF, INC.
and RANDOM HOUSE, INC.

Copyright, 1939, by SIGMUND FREUD. All rights reserved under
International and Pan-American Copyright Conventions.
Copyright renewed, 1967, by ERNST L. FREUD and ANNA FREUD

Manufactured in the United States of America

Contents

Moses and Monotheism

Translator's **Note**

Parts I and II of this book were published in
German in *Imago* in 1937; Part III has not
previously appeared in print.
I am indebted to Mr. James Strachey and
Mr. Wilfred Trotter for kindly reading
through this translation and for making a
number of valuable suggestions. I have also
had the advantage of consulting the author
on some doubtful points. K.J.

Part I. Moses an Egyptian

To deny a people the man whom it praises as the greatest of its sons is not a deed to be undertaken lightheartedly—especially by one belonging to that people. No consideration, however, will move me to set aside truth in favour of supposed national interests. Moreover, the elucidation of the mere facts of the problem may be expected to deepen our insight into the situation with which they are concerned.

The man Moses, the liberator of his people, who gave them their religion and their laws, belonged to an age so remote that the preliminary question arises whether he was a historical person or a legendary figure. If he lived, his time was the thirteenth or fourteenth century B.C.; we have no word of him except from the Holy Books and the written traditions of the Jews. Although the decision lacks final historical certainty, the great majority of historians have expressed the opinion that Moses did live and that the exodus from Egypt, led by him, did in fact take place. It has been maintained with good reason that the later history of Israel could not be understood if this were not admitted. Science today has become much more cautious and deals much more leniently with tradition than it did in the early days of historical investigation.

What first attracts our interest in the person of Moses is his name, which is written Mosche in Hebrew. One may well ask: Where does it come from? What does it mean? As is well known, the story in Exodus, Chapter ii, already answers this question. There we learn that the Egyptian princess who saved the babe from the waters of the Nile gave him his name, adding the etymological explanation: Because I drew him out of the water. But this explanation is obviously inadequate. "The Biblical interpretation of the name: 'He that was drawn out of the water' "—thus an author in the *Jüdisches Lexikon*[1]—"is folk etymology; the active Hebrew form itself of the name (Mosche can at best mean only 'the drawer out') cannot be reconciled with this solution." This argument can be supported by two further reflections: first, that it is nonsensical to credit an Egyptian princess with a knowledge of Hebrew etymology, and, secondly, that the water from which the child was drawn was most probably not the water of the Nile.

On the other hand the suggestion has long been

[1] *Jüdisches Lexikon*, founded by Herlitz and Kirschner, Bd. IV (Berlin: Jüdischer Verlag; 1930).

made and by many different people that the name
Moses derives from the Egyptian vocabulary. Instead
of citing all the authors who have voiced this opinion I
shall quote a passage from a recent work by Breasted,[1]
an author whose *History of Egypt* is regarded as au-
thoritative. "It is important to notice that his name,
Moses, was Egyptian. It is simply the Egyptian word
'mose' meaning 'child,' and is an abridgement of a
fuller form of such names as 'Amen-mose' meaning
'Amon-a-child' or 'Ptah-mose,' meaning 'Ptah-a-child,'
these forms themselves being likewise abbreviations
for the complete form 'Amon- (has-given) -a-child' or
'Ptah- (has-given) -a-child.' The abbreviation 'child'
early became a convenient rapid form for the cum-
brous full name, and the name Mose, 'child,' is not un-
common on the Egyptian monuments. The father of
Moses without doubt prefixed to his son's name that
of an Egyptian god like Amon or Ptah, and this divine
name was gradually lost in current usage, till the boy
was called 'Mose.' (The final *s* is an addition drawn
from the Greek translation of the Old Testament. It
is not in the Hebrew, which has 'mosheh')." I have
given this passage literally and am by no means prepared to share the responsibility for its details. I am
a little surprised, however, that Breasted in citing
related names should have passed over the analogous
theophorous names in the list of Egyptian kings, such
as Ah-mose, Thut-mose (Thotmes), and Ra-mose
(Ramses).

It might have been expected that one of the

[1] *The Dawn of Conscience* (New York: Charles Scribner's
Sons; 1934), p. 350.

many authors who recognized Moses to be an Egyptian name would have drawn the conclusion, or at least considered the possibility, that the bearer of an Egyptian name was himself an Egyptian. In modern times we have no misgiving in drawing such conclusions, although today a person bears two names, not one, and although a change of name or assimilation of it in new conditions cannot be ruled out. So we are not at all surprised to find that the poet Chamisso was of French extraction, Napoleon Buonaparte, on the other hand, of Italian, and that Benjamin Disraeli was an Italian Jew, as his name would lead us to expect. And such an inference from the name to the race should be more reliable and indeed conclusive in respect of early and primitive times. Nevertheless to the best of my knowledge no historian has drawn this conclusion in the case of Moses, not even one of those who, like Breasted, are ready to suppose that Moses "was cognizant of all the wisdom of the Egyptians." [1]

What hindered them from doing so can only be guessed at. Perhaps the awe of Biblical tradition was insuperable. Perhaps it seemed monstrous to imagine that the man Moses could have been anything other than a Hebrew. In any event, what happened was that the recognition of the name being Egyptian was not a factor in judging the origin of the man Moses, and that nothing further was deduced from it. If the question of the nationality of this great man is considered important, then any new material for answering it must be welcome.

This is what my little essay attempts. The con-

[1] Op. cit., p. 334.

tribution it brings is an application of psychoanalysis. The considerations thus reached will impress only that minority of readers familiar with analytical reasoning and able to appreciate its conclusions. To them I hope it will appear of significance.

In 1909 Otto Rank, then still under my influence, published at my suggestion a book entitled: *Der Mythus von der Geburt des Helden.*[1] It deals with the fact "that almost all important civilized peoples have early woven myths around and glorified in poetry their heroes, mythical kings and princes, founders of religions, of dynasties, empires and cities—in short, their national heroes. Especially the history of their birth and of their early years is furnished with phantastic traits; the amazing similarity, nay, literal identity, of those tales, even if they refer to different, completely independent peoples, sometimes geographically far removed from one another, is well known and has struck many an investigator." Following Rank we reconstruct—on the lines of Galton's technique—an "average myth" that makes prominent the essential features of all these tales, and we then get this formula:

"The hero is the son of parents of the highest station, most often the son of a king.

"His conception is impeded by difficulties, such as abstinence or temporary sterility; or else his parents practise intercourse in secret because of prohibitions or other external obstacles. During his mother's preg-

---

[1] *Schriften zur angewandten Seelenkunde* (Vienna: F. Deuticke), Heft 5. It is far from my mind to depreciate the value of Rank's original contributions to this work.

nancy or earlier an oracle or a dream warns the father of the child's birth as containing grave danger for his safety.

"In consequence the father (or a person representing him) gives orders for the new-born babe to be killed or exposed to extreme danger; in most cases the babe is placed in a casket and delivered to the waves.

"The child is then saved by animals or poor people, such as shepherds, and suckled by a female animal or a woman of humble birth.

"When full grown he rediscovers his noble parents after many strange adventures, wreaks vengeance on his father, and, recognized by his people, attains fame and greatness."

The most remote of the historical personages to whom this myth attaches is Sargon of Agade, the founder of Babylon about 2800 B.C. From the point of view of what interests us here it would perhaps be worth while to reproduce the account ascribed to himself:

"I am Sargon, the mighty king, King of Agade. My mother was a vestal; my father I knew not; while my father's brother dwelt in the mountains. In my town Azupirani—it lies on the banks of Euphrates—my mother, the vestal, conceived me. *Secretly she bore me. She laid me in a basket of sedge,* closed the opening with pitch, and *lowered me into the river.* The stream did not drown me, but carried me to Akki, the drawer of water. Akki, the drawer of water, in the goodness of his heart lifted me out of the water, *Akki, the drawer of water, as his own son he brought me up.*

Akki, the drawer of water, made me his gardener. When I was a gardener, Istar fell in love with me. I became king and for forty-five years I ruled as king."

The best-known names in the series beginning with Sargon of Agade are Moses, Cyrus, and Romulus. But besides these Rank has enumerated many other heroes belonging to myth or poetry to whom the same youthful story attaches either in its entirety or in well-recognizable parts, such as Œdipus, Karna, Paris, Telephos, Perseus, Heracles, Gilgamesh, Amphion, Zethos, and others.

The source and the tendency of such myths are familiar to us through Rank's work. I need only refer to his conclusions with a few short hints. A hero is a man who stands up manfully against his father and in the end victoriously overcomes him. The myth in question traces this struggle back to the very dawn of the hero's life, by having him born against his father's will and saved in spite of his father's evil intentions. The exposure in the basket is clearly a symbolical representation of birth; the basket is the womb, the stream the water at birth. In innumerable dreams the relation of the child to the parents is represented by drawing or saving from the water. When the imagination of a people attaches this myth to a famous personage it is to indicate that he is recognized as a hero, that his life has conformed to the typical plan. The inner source of the myth is the so-called "family romance" of the child, in which the son reacts to the change in his inner relationship to his parents, especially that to his father. The child's first years are governed by grandiose over-estimation of his father·

kings and queens in dreams and fairytales always represent, accordingly, the parents. Later on, under the influence of rivalry and real disappointments, the release from the parents and a critical attitude towards the father set in. The two families of the myth, the noble as well as the humble one, are therefore both images of his own family as they appear to the child in successive periods of his life.

It is not too much to say that these observations fully explain the similarity as well as the far-spread occurrence of the myth of the birth of the hero. It is all the more interesting to find that the myth of Moses' birth and exposure stands apart; in one essential point it even contradicts the others.

We start with the two families between which the myth has cast the child's fate. We know that analytic interpretation makes them into one family, that the distinction is only a temporal one. In the typical form of the myth the first family, into which the child is born, is a noble and mostly a royal one; the second family, in which the child grows up, is a humble and degraded one, corresponding with the circumstances to which the interpretation refers. Only in the story of Œdipus is this difference obscured. The babe exposed by one kingly family is brought up by another royal pair. It can hardly be an accident that in this one example there is in the myth itself a glimmer of the original identity of the two families. The social contrast of the two families—meant, as we know, to stress the heroic nature of a great man—gives a second function to our myth, which becomes especially significant with historical personages. It can also be used to provide for our hero a patent of nobility to elevate him to a higher social rank. Thus Cyrus is for the Medes an alien conqueror; by way of the exposure myth he becomes the grandson of their king. A similar trait occurs in the myth of Romulus; if such a man ever lived he must have been an unknown adventurer, an upstart; the myth makes him a descendant of, and heir to, the royal house of Alba Longa.

It is very different in the case of Moses. Here the first family—usually so distinguished—is modest enough. He is the child of Jewish Levites. But the second family—the humble one in which as a rule heroes are brought up—is replaced by the royal house of Egypt; the princess brings him up as her own son. This divergence from the usual type has struck many research workers as strange. Eduard Meyer and others after him supposed the original form of the myth to have been different. Pharaoh had been warned by a prophetic dream[1] that his daughter's son would become a danger to him and his kingdom. This is why he has the child delivered to the waters of the Nile shortly after his birth. But the child is saved by Jewish people and brought up as their own. "National motives," in Rank's terminology,[2] had transformed the myth into the form now known by us.

However, further thought tells us that an original Moses myth of this kind, one not diverging from other birth myths, could not have existed. For the legend is either of Egyptian or of Jewish origin. The

---

[1] Also mentioned in Flavius Josephus's narration.
[2] Loc. cit., p. 80, footnote.

first supposition may be excluded. The Egyptians had no motive to glorify Moses; to them he was not a hero. So the legend should have originated among the Jewish people; that is to say, it was attached in the usual version to the person of their leader. But for that purpose it was entirely unfitted; what good is a legend to a people that makes their hero into an alien?

The Moses myth as we know it today lags sadly behind its secret motives. If Moses is not of royal lineage our legend cannot make him into a hero; if he remains a Jew it has done nothing to raise his status. Only one small feature of the whole myth remains effective: the assurance that the babe survived in spite of strong outside forces to the contrary. This feature is repeated in the early history of Jesus, where King Herod assumes the role of Pharaoh. So we really have a right to assume that in a later and rather clumsy treatment of the legendary material the adapter saw fit to equip his hero Moses with certain features appertaining to the classical exposure myths characteristic of a hero, and yet unsuited to Moses by reason of the special circumstances.

With this unsatisfactory and even uncertain result our investigation would have to end, without having contributed anything to answering the question whether Moses was Egyptian, were there not another and perhaps more successful way of approaching the exposure myth itself.

Let us return to the two families in the myth. As we know, on the level of analytic interpretation they are identical. On a mythical level they are distinguished as the noble and the humble family. With a historical person to whom the myth has become attached there is, however, a third level, that of reality. One of the families is the real one, the one into which the great man was really born and in which he was brought up. The other is fictitious, invented by the myth in pursuance of its own motives. As a rule the real family corresponds with the humble one, the noble family with the fictitious one. In the case of Moses something seemed to be different. And here the new point of view may perhaps bring some illumination. It is that the first family, the one from which the babe is exposed to danger, is in all comparable cases the fictitious one; the second family, however, by which the hero is adopted and in which he grows up, is his real one. If we have the courage to accept this statement as a general truth to which the Moses legend also is subject, then we suddenly see our way clear. Moses is an Egyptian—probably of noble origin— whom the myth undertakes to transform into a Jew. And that would be our conclusion! The exposure in the water was in its right place; to fit the new conclusion the intention had to be changed, not without violence. From a means of getting rid of the child it becomes a means of its salvation.

The divergence of the Moses legend from all others of its kind might be traced back to a special feature in the story of Moses' life. Whereas in all other cases the hero rises above his humble beginnings as his life progresses, the heroic life of the man Moses began by descending from his eminence to the level of the children of Israel.

This little investigation was undertaken in the

hope of gaining from it a second, fresh argument for the suggestion that Moses was an Egyptian. We have seen that the first argument, that of his name, has not been considered decisive.[1] We have to be prepared for the new reasoning—the analysis of the exposure myth—not faring any better. The objection is likely to be that the circumstances of the origin and transformation of legends are too obscure to allow of such a conclusion as the preceding one, and that all efforts to extract the kernel of historical truth must be doomed to failure in face of the incoherence and contradictions clustering around the heroic person of Moses and the unmistakable signs of tendentious distortion and stratification accumulated through many centuries. I myself do not share this negative attitude, but I am not in a position to confute it.

If there was no more certainty than this to be attained, why have I brought this inquiry to the notice of a wider public? I regret that even my justification has to restrict itself to hints. If, however, one is attracted by the two arguments outlined above and tries to take seriously the conclusion that Moses was a distinguished Egyptian, then very interesting and far-reaching perspectives open out. With the help of certain assumptions the motives guiding Moses in his unusual undertaking can be made intelligible; in close

---

[1] Thus E. Meyer in *"Die Mosessagen und die Lewiten,"* in *Sitzungsberichte der königlich preussischen Akademie der Wissenschaften* (Berlin, 1905): "The name Mose is probably the name Pinchas in the priest dynasty of Silo .. without a doubt Egyptian. This does not prove, however, that these dynasties were of Egyptian origin, but it proves that they had relations with Egypt" (p. 651). One may well ask what kind of relations one is to imagine.

connection with this the possible motivation of numerous characteristics and peculiarities of the legislation and religion he gave the Jewish people can be perceived. It stimulates ideas of some moment concerning the origin of monotheistic religion in general. But such important considerations cannot be based on psychological probabilities alone. Even if one were to accept it as historical that Moses was Egyptian, we should want at least one other fixed point so as to protect the many emerging possibilities from the reproach of their being products of imagination and too far removed from reality. An objective proof of the period into which the life of Moses, and with it the exodus from Egypt, fall would perhaps have sufficed. But this has not been forthcoming, and therefore it will be better to suppress any inferences that might follow our view that Moses was an Egyptian.

In Part I of this book I have tried to strengthen by a new argument the suggestion that the man Moses, the liberator and lawgiver of the Jewish people, was not a Jew, but an Egyptian. That his name derived from the Egyptian vocabulary had long been observed, though not duly appreciated. I added to this consideration the further one that the interpretation of the exposure myth attaching to Moses necessitated the conclusion that he was an Egyptian whom a people needed to make into a Jew. At the end of my essay I said that important and far-reaching conclusions could be drawn from the suggestion that Moses was an Egyptian; but I was not prepared to uphold them publicly, since they were based only on psychological probabilities and lacked objective proof. The more significant the possibilities thus discerned, the more cautious is one about exposing them to the critical attack of the outside world without any secure foundation—like an iron monument with feet of clay. No probability, however seductive, can protect us from error; even if all parts of a problem seem to fit together like the pieces of a jigsaw puzzle, one has to remember that the probable need not necessarily be the truth, and the truth not always probable. And, lastly, it is not attractive to be classed with the scholastics and Talmudists who are satisfied to exercise their ingenuity, unconcerned how far removed their conclusions may be from the truth.

Notwithstanding these misgivings, which weigh as heavily today as they did then, out of the conflict of my motives the decision has emerged to follow up my first essay by this contribution. But once again it is only a part of the whole, and not the most important part.

I

If, then, Moses was an Egyptian, the first gain from this suggestion is a new riddle, one difficult to answer. When a people of a tribe[1] prepares for a great undertaking, it is to be expected that one of them should make himself their leader or be chosen for this role. But what could have induced a distinguished Egyptian—perhaps a prince, priest, or high

[1] We have no inkling what numbers were concerned in the Exodus.

official—to place himself at the head of a throng of culturally inferior immigrants, and to leave the country with them, is not easy to conjecture. The well-known contempt of the Egyptians for foreigners makes such a proceeding especially unlikely. Indeed, I am inclined to think this is why even those historians who recognized the name as Egyptian, and ascribed all the wisdom of Egypt to him, were not willing to entertain the obvious possibility that Moses was an Egyptian.

      This first difficulty is followed by a second. We must not forget that Moses was not only the political leader of the Jews settled in Egypt, he was also their lawgiver and educator and the man who forced them to adopt a new religion, which is still today called Mosaic after him. But can a single person create a new religion so easily? And when someone wishes to influence the religion of another, would not the most natural thing be to convert him to his own? The Jewish people in Egypt were certainly not without some kind of religion, and if Moses, who gave them a new religion, was an Egyptian, then the surmise cannot be rejected that this other new religion was the Egyptian one.

  This possibility encounters an obstacle: the sharp contrast between the Jewish religion attributed to Moses and the Egyptian one. The former is a grandiosely rigid monotheism. There is only one God, unique, omnipotent, unapproachable. The sight of his countenance cannot be borne; one must not make an image of him, nor even breathe his name. In the Egyptian religion, on the other hand, there is a bewildering mass of deities of differing importance and provenance. Some of them are personifications of great natural powers like heaven and earth, sun and moon. Then we find an abstraction such as Maat (Justice, Truth) or a grotesque creature like the dwarfish Bes. Most of them, however, are local gods from the time when the land was divided into numerous provinces. They have the shapes of animals as if they had not yet overcome their origin in the old totem animals. They are not clearly differentiated, barely distinguished by special functions attributed to some of them. The hymns in praise of these gods tell the same thing about each of them, identify them with one another without any misgivings, in a way that would confuse us hopelessly. Names of deities are combined with one another, so that one becomes degraded almost to an epithet of the other. Thus in the best period of the "New Empire" the main god of the city of Thebes is called Amon-Re, in which combination the first part signifies the ram-headed city-god, whereas Re is the name of the hawk-headed sun-god of On. Magic and ceremonial, amulets and formulas dominated the service of these gods, as they did the daily life of the Egyptians.

Some of these differences may easily derive from the contrast in principle between a strict monotheism and an unlimited polytheism. Others are obviously consequences of a difference in intellectual level; one religion is very near to the primitive, the other has soared to the heights of sublime abstraction. Perhaps it is these two characteristics that occasionally give one the impression that the contrast between the Mosaic and the Egyptian religion is one intended and pur-

posely accentuated; for example, when the one religion severely condemns any kind of magic or sorcery,
which flourishes so abundantly in the other; or when
the insatiable zest of the Egyptian for making images
of his gods in clay, stone, and metal, to which our
museums owe so much, is contrasted with the way in
which the making of the image of any living or vision-
ary being is bluntly forbidden.

There is yet another difference between the
two religions which the explanations I have attempted
do not touch. No other people of antiquity has done
so much to deny death, has made such careful provi-
sion for an after-life; in accordance with this the
death-god Osiris, the ruler of that other world, was
the most popular and indisputable of all Egyptian
gods. The early Jewish religion, on the other hand,
had entirely relinquished immortality; the possibility
of an existence after death was never mentioned in
any place. And this is all the more remarkable since
later experience has shown that the belief in a life
beyond can very well be reconciled with a monotheistic religion.

I had hoped the suggestion that Moses was an
Egyptian would prove enlightening and stimulating in
many different respects. But our first deduction from
this suggestion—that the new religion he gave the
Jews was his own, the Egyptian one—has foundered
on the difference—nay, the striking contrast—between
the two religions.

II

A strange fact in the history of the Egyptian religion, which was recognized and appraised relatively late, opens up another point of view. It is still possible that the religion Moses gave to his Jewish people was yet his own, *an* Egyptian religion though not *the* Egyptian one.

In the glorious Eighteenth Dynasty, when Egypt became for the first time a world power, a young Pharaoh ascended the throne about 1375 B.C., who first called himself Amenhotep (IV) like his father, but later on changed his name—and not only his name. This king undertook to force upon his subjects a new religion, one contrary to their ancient traditions and to all their familiar habits. It was a strict monotheism, the first attempt of its kind in the history of the world, as far as we know; and religious intolerance, which was foreign to antiquity before this and for long after, was inevitably born with the belief in one God. But Amenhotep's reign lasted only for seventeen years; very soon after his death in 1358 the new religion was swept away and the memory of the heretic king proscribed. From the ruins of his new capital, which he had built and dedicated to his God, and from the inscriptions in the rock tombs belonging to it, we derive the little knowledge we possess of him. Everything we can learn about this remarkable, indeed unique person is worthy of the greatest interest.[1]

[1] Breasted called him "the first individual in human history."

Everything new must have its roots in what was before. The origin of Egyptian monotheism can be traced back a fair distance with some certainty.[1] In the School of Priests in the Sun Temple at On (Heliopolis) tendencies had for some time been at work developing the idea of a universal god and stressing his ethical aspects. Maat, the goddess of truth, order, and justice, was a daughter of the sun-god, Re. Already under Amenhotep III, the father and predecessor of the reformer, the worship of the sun-god was in the ascendant, probably in opposition to the worship of Amon of Thebes, who had become over-prominent. An ancient name of the sun-god, Aton or Atum, was rediscovered, and in this Aton religion the young king found a movement he had no need to create, but one which he could join.

Political conditions in Egypt had about that time begun to exert a lasting influence on Egyptian religion. Through the victorious sword of the great conqueror Thothmes III Egypt had become a world power. Nubia in the south, Palestine, Syria, and a part of Mesopotamia in the north had been added to the Empire. This imperialism was reflected in religion as universality and monotheism. Since Pharaoh's solicitude now extended beyond Egypt to Nubia and Syria, deity itself had to give up its national limitation, and the new god of the Egyptians had to become like Pharaoh—the unique and unlimited sovereign of the world known to the Egyptians. Besides, it

[1] The account I give here follows closely J. H. Breasted's *History of Egypt* (1906) and *The Dawn of Conscience* (1934), and the corresponding sections in *The Cambridge Ancient History*, Vol. II.

was natural that as the frontiers extended, Egypt should become accessible to foreign influences; some of the king's wives were Asiatic princesses,[1] and possibly even direct encouragement of monotheism had penetrated from Syria.

Amenhotep never denied his accession to the sun cult of On. In the two hymns to Aton which have been preserved to us through the inscriptions in the rock tombs and which were probably composed by him, he praises the sun as the creator and preserver of all living beings in and outside Egypt with a fervour such as recurs many centuries after only in the psalms in honour of the Jewish God, Jahve. But he did not stop at this astonishing anticipation of scientific knowledge concerning the effect of sunlight. There is no doubt that he went further: that he worshipped the sun not as a material object, but as a symbol of a divine being whose energy was manifested in his rays.[2]

But we do scant justice to the king if we see in him only the adherent and protector of an Atón religion which had already existed before him. His ac-

---

[1] Perhaps even Amenhotep's beloved spouse Nofertete.

[2] Breasted: *History of Egypt*, p. 360: "But however evident the Heliopolitan origin of the new state religion might be, it was not merely sun-worship; the word Aton was employed in the place of the old word for 'god' (nuter), and the god is clearly distinguished from the material sun." "It is evident that what the king was deifying was the force by which the Sun made itself felt on earth" (*Dawn of Conscience*, p. 279). Erman's opinion of a formula in honour of the god is similar (A. Erman: *Die Ægyptische Religion;* 1905): "There are . . . words which are meant to express in an abstract form the fact that not the star itself was worshipped, but the Being that manifested itself in it."

tivity was much more energetic. He added the something new that turned into monotheism the doctrine
of a universal god: the quality of exclusiveness. In
one of his hymns it is stated in so many words: "O
Thou only God, there is no other God than Thou." [1]
And we must not forget that to appraise the new
doctrine it is not enough to know its positive content
only; nearly as important is its negative side, the
knowledge of what it repudiates. It would be a mis-
take, too, to suppose that the new religion sprang to
life ready and fully equipped like Athene out of Zeus'
forehead. Everything rather goes to show that during
Amenhotep's reign it was strengthened so as to attain
greater clarity, consistency, harshness, and intolerance.
Probably this development took place under the influence of the violent opposition among the priests of
Amon that raised its head against the reforms of the
king. In the sixth year of Amenhotep's reign this
enmity had grown to such an extent that the king
changed his name, of which the now proscribed name
of the god Amon was a part. Instead of Amenhotep
he called himself Ikhnaton.[2] But not only from his
name did he eliminate that of the hated god, but also
from all inscriptions and even where he found it in
his father's name, Amenhotep III. Soon after his
change of name Ikhnaton left Thebes, which was under Amon's rule, and built a new capital lower down

---

[1] Breasted: *History of Egypt*, p. 374.

[2] I follow Breasted's spelling of this name (sometimes
spelled Akhenaton). The king's new name means approximately
the same as his former one: "God is satisfied." Compare the
English Godfrey and the German Gotthold.

the river, which he called Akhetaton (Horizon of Aton). Its ruins are now called Tell-el-Amarna.[1]

The persecution by the king was directed foremost against Amon, but not against him alone. Everywhere in the Empire the temples were closed, the services forbidden, and the ecclesiastical property seized. Indeed, the king's zeal went so far as to cause an inquiry to be made into the inscriptions on old monuments in order to efface the word "God" whenever it was used in the plural.[2] It is not to be wondered at that these orders produced a reaction of fanatical vengeance among the suppressed priests and the discontented people, a reaction which was able to find a free outlet after the king's death. The Aton religion had not appealed to the people; it had probably been limited to a small circle round Ikhnaton's person. His end is wrapped in mystery. We learn of a few short-lived, shadowy successors of his own family. Already his son-in-law Tutankhaton was forced to return to Thebes and to substitute Amon in his name for the god Aton. Then there followed a period of anarchy until the general Haremhab succeeded in 1350 B.C. in restoring order. The glorious Eighteenth Dynasty was extinguished; at the same time its conquests in Nubia and Asia were lost. In this sad interregnum Egypt's old religions had been reinstated. The Aton religion was at an end, Ikhnaton's capital lay de-

---

[1] This is where in 1887 the correspondence of the Egyptian kings with their friends and vassals in Asia was found, a correspondence which proved so important for our knowledge of history.

[2] Idem, *History of Egypt*, p. 363.

stroyed and plundered, and his memory was scorned as that of a felon.

It will serve a certain purpose if we now note several negative characteristics of the Aton religion. In the first place, all myth, magic, and sorcery are excluded from it.[1]

Then there is the way in which the sun-god is represented: no longer as in earlier times by a small pyramid and a falcon, but—and this is almost rational —by a round disk from which emanate rays terminating in human hands. In spite of all the love for art in the Amarna period, not one personal representation of the sun-god Aton has been found, or, we may say with confidence, ever will be found.[2]

Finally, there is a complete silence about the death-god Osiris and the realm of the dead. Neither hymns nor inscriptions on graves know anything of what was perhaps nearest to the Egyptian's heart. The contrast with the popular religion cannot be expressed more vividly.[3]

[1] Arthur Weigall (*The Life and Times of Akhnaton*, 1923, p. 121) says that Ikhnaton would not recognize a hell against the terrors of which one had to guard by innumerable magic spells. "Akhnaton flung all these formulas into the fire. Djins, bogies, spirits, monsters, demigods and Osiris himself with all his court, were swept into the blaze and reduced to ashes."

[2] Weigall, op. cit., p. 103: "Akhnaton did not permit any graven image to be made of the Aton. The true God, said the King, had no form; and he held to this opinion throughout his life."

[3] Erman, op. cit., p. 90: "Of Osiris and his realm no more was to be heard." Breasted: *Dawn of Conscience*, p. 291. "Osiris is completely ignored. He is never mentioned in any record of Ikhnaton or in any of the tombs at Amarna."

III

I venture now to draw the following conclusion: if Moses was an Egyptian and if he transmitted to the Jews his own religion, then it was that of Ikhnaton, the Aton religion.

I compared earlier the Jewish religion with the religion of the Egyptian people and noted how different they were from each other. Now we shall compare the Jewish with the Aton religion and should expect to find that they were originally identical. We know that this is no easy task. Of the Aton religion we do not perhaps know enough, thanks to the revengeful spirit of the Amon priests. The Mosaic religion we know only in its final form as it was fixed by Jewish priests in the time after the Exile, about eight hundred years later. If, in spite of this unpromising material, we should find some indications fitting in with our supposition, then we may indeed value them highly.

There would be a short way of proving our thesis that the Mosaic religion is nothing else but that of Aton: namely, by a confession of faith, a proclamation. But I am afraid I should be told that such a road is impracticable. The Jewish creed, as is well known, says: *"Schema Jisroel Adonai Elohenu Adonai Echod."* If the similarity of the name of the Egyptian Aton (or Atum) to the Hebrew word Adonai and the Syrian divine name Adonis is not a mere accident, but is the result of a primeval unity in language and meaning, then one could translate the Jewish formula: "Hear, O Israel, our God Aton (Adonai) is the only God." I am, alas, entirely unqualified to answer this question and have been able to find very little about it in the literature concerned,[1] but probably we had better not make things so simple. Moreover, we shall have to come back to the problems of the divine name.

The points of similarity as well as those of difference in the two religions are easily discerned, but do not enlighten us much. Both are forms of a strict monotheism, and we shall be inclined to reduce to this basic character what is similar in both of them. Jewish monotheism is in some points even more uncompromising than the Egyptian—for example, when it forbids all visual representation of its God. The most essential difference—apart from the name of its God—is that the Jewish religion entirely relinquishes the worship of the sun, to which the Egyptian one still adhered. When comparing the Jewish with the Egyptian folk religion we received the impression that, besides the contrast in principle, there was in the difference between the two religions an element of purposive contradiction. This impression appears justified when in our comparison we replace the Jewish religion by that of Aton, which Ikhnaton, as we know, developed in deliberate antagonism to the popular religion. We were astonished—and rightly so

[1] Only a few passages in Weigall, op. cit., pp. 12, 19: "The god Atum, who described Re as the setting sun, was perhaps of the same origin as Aton, generally venerated in Northern Syria. A foreign Queen, as well as her suite, might therefore have been attracted to Heliopolis rather than to Thebes."

—that the Jewish religion did not speak of anything beyond the grave, for such a doctrine is reconcilable with the strictest monotheism. This astonishment disappears if we go back from the Jewish religion to the Aton religion and surmise that this feature was taken over from the latter, since for Ikhnaton it was a necessity in fighting the popular religion, where the death-god Osiris played perhaps a greater part than any god of the upper regions. The agreement of the Jewish religion with that of Aton in this important point is the first strong argument in favour of our thesis. We shall see that it is not the only one.

Moses gave the Jews not only a new religion; it is equally certain that he introduced the custom of circumcision. This has a decisive importance for our problem and it has hardly ever been weighed. The Biblical account, it is true, often contradicts it. On the one hand, it dates the custom back to the time of the patriarchs as a sign of the covenant concluded between God and Abraham. On the other hand, the text mentions in an especially obscure passage that God was wroth with Moses because he had neglected this holy usage, and proposed to slay him as a punishment. Moses' wife, a Midianite, saved her husband from the wrath of God by speedily performing the operation. These are distortions, however, which should not lead us astray; we shall explore their motives presently. The fact remains that the question concerning the origin of circumcision has only one answer: it comes from Egypt. Herodotus, "the Father of History," tells us that the custom of circumcision had long been practised in Egypt, and his statement has been confirmed by the examination of mummies and even by drawings on the walls of graves. No other people of the eastern Mediterranean, as far as we know, has followed this custom; we can assume with certainty that the Semites, Babylonians, and Sumerians were not circumcised. Biblical history itself says as much of the inhabitants of Canaan; it is presupposed in the story of the adventure between Jacob's daughter and the Prince of Shechem.[1] The possibility that the Jews in Egypt adopted the usage of circumcision in any other way than in connection with the religion Moses gave them may be rejected as quite untenable. Now let us bear in mind that circumcision was practised in Egypt by the people as a general custom, and let us adopt for the moment the usual assumption that Moses was a Jew who wanted to free his compatriots from the service of an Egyptian overlord and lead them out of the country to develop an independent and self-confident existence—a feat he actually achieved. What sense could there be in his forcing upon them at the same time a burdensome custom which, so to speak, made them into Egyptians and was bound to keep awake their memory of Egypt,

---

[1] When I use Biblical tradition here in such an autocratic and arbitrary way, draw on it for confirmation whenever it is convenient, and dismiss its evidence without scruple when it contradicts my conclusions, I know full well that I am exposing myself to severe criticism concerning my method and that I weaken the force of my proofs. But this is the only way in which to treat material whose trustworthiness—as we know for certain —was seriously damaged by the influence of distorting tendencies. Some justification will be forthcoming later, it is hoped, when we have unearthed those secret motives. Certainty is not to be gained in any case, and, moreover, we may say that all other authors have acted likewise.

whereas his intention could only have had the opposite aim: namely, that his people should become strangers to the country of bondage and overcome the longing for the "fleshpots of Egypt"? No, the fact we started from and the suggestion I added to it are so incompatible with each other that I venture to draw the following conclusion: If Moses gave the Jews not only a new religion, but also the law of circumcision, he was no Jew, but an Egyptian, and then the Mosaic religion was probably an Egyptian one: namely—because of its contrast to the popular religion—that of Aton, with which the Jewish one shows agreement in some remarkable points.

As I remarked earlier, my hypothesis that Moses was not a Jew, but an Egyptian, creates a new enigma. What he did—easily understandable if he were a Jew—becomes unintelligible in an Egyptian. But if we place Moses in Ikhnaton's period and associate him with that Pharaoh, then the enigma is resolved and a possible motive presents itself, answering all our questions. Let us assume that Moses was a noble and distinguished man, perhaps indeed a member of the royal house, as the myth has it. He must have been conscious of his great abilities, ambitious, and energetic; perhaps he saw himself in a dim future as the leader of his people, the governor of the Empire. In close contact with Pharaoh, he was a convinced adherent of the new religion, whose basic principles he fully understood and had made his own. With the king's death and the subsequent reaction he saw all his hopes and prospects destroyed. If he was not to recant the convictions so dear to him, then Egypt had no more to give him; he had lost his native country. In this hour of need he found an unusual solution. The dreamer Ikhnaton had estranged himself from his people, had let his world empire crumble. Moses' active nature conceived the plan of founding a new empire, of finding a new people, to whom he could give the religion that Egypt disdained. It was, as we perceive, a heroic attempt to struggle against his fate, to find compensation in two directions for the losses he had suffered through Ikhnaton's catastrophe. Perhaps he was at the time governor of that border province (Gosen) in which—perhaps already in "the Hyksos period"—certain Semitic tribes had settled. These he chose to be his new people. A historic decision! [1]

He established relations with them, placed himself at their head, and directed the Exodus "by strength of hand." In full contradistinction to the Biblical tradition we may suppose this Exodus to have passed off peacefully and without pursuit. The authority of Moses made it possible, and there was then no central power that could have prevented it.

According to our construction the Exodus from Egypt would have taken place between 1358 and 1350 B.C.—that is to say, after the death of Ikhnaton and *before* the restitution of the authority of the state

[1] If Moses were a high official, we can understand his being fitted for the role of leader he assumed with the Jews. If he were a priest, the thought of giving his people a new religion must have been near to his heart. In both cases he would have continued his former profession. A prince of royal lineage might easily have been both: governor and priest. In the report of Flavius Josephus (*Jewish Antiquities*), who accepts the exposure myth, but seems to know other traditions than the Biblical one, Moses appears as an Egyptian field-marshal in a victorious campaign in Ethiopia.

by Haremhab.[1] The goal of the wandering could only be Canaan. After the supremacy of Egypt had collapsed, hordes of warlike Aramæans had flooded the country, conquering and pillaging, and thus had shown where a capable people could seize new land. We know these warriors from the letters which were found in 1887 in the archives of the ruined city of Amarna. There they are called Habiru, and the name was passed on—no one knows how—to the Jewish invaders, Hebrews, who came later and could not have been referred to in the letters of Amarna. The tribes who were the most nearly related to the Jews now leaving Egypt also lived south of Palestine—in Canaan.

The motivation that we have surmised for the Exodus as a whole covers also the institution of circumcision. We know in what manner human beings—both peoples and individuals—react to this ancient custom, scarcely any longer understood. Those who do not practise it regard it as very odd and find it rather abhorrent; but those who have adopted circumcision are proud of the custom. They feel superior, ennobled, and look down with contempt on the others, who appear to them unclean. Even today the Turk hurls abuse at the Christian by calling him "an uncircumcised dog." It is credible that Moses, who as an Egyptian was himself circumcised, shared this attitude. The Jews with whom he left his native country were to be a better substitute for the Egyptians he

[1] This would be about a century earlier than most historians assume, who place it in the Nineteenth Dynasty under Merneptah; or perhaps a little less, for official records seem to include the interregnum in Haremhab's reign.

left behind. In no circumstances must they be inferior
to them. He wished to make of them a "holy nation"
—so it is explicitly stated in the Biblical text—and as
a sign of their dedication he introduced the custom
that made them at least the equals of the Egyptians.
It would, further, be welcome to him if such a custom
isolated them and prevented them from mingling with
the other foreign peoples they would meet during
their wanderings, just as the Egyptians had kept apart
from all foreigners.[1]

Jewish tradition, however, behaved later on as
if it were oppressed by the sequence of ideas we have
just developed. To admit that circumcision was an
Egyptian custom introduced by Moses would be almost to recognize that the religion handed down to
them from Moses was also Egyptian. But the Jews had

---

[1] Herodotus, who visited Egypt about 450 B.C., gives in
the account of his travels a characteristic of the Egyptians which
shows an astounding similarity with well-known features of the
later Jewish people. "They are in all respects much more pious
than other peoples. They are also distinguished from them by
many of their customs, such as circumcision, which for reasons
of cleanliness they introduced before others; further, by their
horror of swine, doubtless connected with the fact that Set
wounded Horus when in the guise of a black hog; and, lastly,
most of all by their reverence for cows, which they would never
eat or sacrifice because they would thereby offend the cow-horned
Isis. Therefore no Egyptian man or woman would ever kiss a
Greek or use his knife, his spit, or his cooking vessel, or eat of
the meat of an (otherwise) clean ox that had been cut with a
Greek knife. . . . In haughty narrowness they looked down on
the other peoples who were unclean and not so near to the gods
as they were." (After Erman: *Die Ægyptische Religion*, pp.
181 ff.)

Naturally, we do not forget here the parallels from the
life of India. What ever gave, by the way, the Jewish poet Heine
in the nineteenth century the idea of complaining about his
religion as "the plague trailing along from the valley of the
Nile, the sickly beliefs of the ancient Egyptians"?

good reasons to deny this fact; therefore the truth
about circumcision had also to be contradicted.

IV

At this point I expect to hear the reproach that
I have built up my construction—which places Moses
the Egyptian in Ikhnaton's era, derives from the political state the country was in at that time his decision
to protect the Jewish people, and recognizes as the
Aton religion the religion he gave to his people or
with which he burdened them, which had just been
abolished in Egypt itself—that I have built up this
edifice of conjectures with too great a certainty, for
which no adequate grounds are to be found in the
material itself. I think this reproach would be unjustified. I have already stressed the element of doubt
in the introduction, put a query in front of the brackets, so to speak, and can therefore save myself the
trouble of repeating it at each point inside the
brackets.

Some of my own critical observations may continue the discussion. The kernel of our thesis, the dependence of Jewish monotheism on the monotheistic
episode in Egyptian history, has been guessed and
hinted at by several workers. I need not cite them
here, since none of them has been able to say by what
means this influence was exerted. Even if, as I suggest,
it is bound up with the individuality of Moses, we
shall have to weigh other possibilities than the one
here preferred. It is not to be supposed that the over-

throw of the official Aton religion completely put an end to the monotheistic trend in Egypt. The School of Priests at On, from which it emanated, survived the catastrophe and might have drawn whole generations after Ikhnaton into the orbit of their religious thought. That Moses performed the deed is quite thinkable, therefore, even if he did not live in Ikhnaton's time and had not come under his personal influence, even if he were simply an adherent or merely a member of the school of On. This conjecture would postpone the date of the Exodus and bring it nearer to the time usually assumed, the thirteenth century B.C.; otherwise it has nothing to recommend it. We should have to relinquish the insight we had gained into Moses' motives and to dispense with the idea of the Exodus being facilitated by the anarchy prevailing in Egypt. The kings of the Nineteenth Dynasty following Ikhnaton ruled the country with a strong hand. All conditions, internal and external, favouring the Exodus coincide only in the period immediately after the death of the heretic king.

The Jews possess a rich extra-Biblical literature in which are to be found the myths and superstitions that in the course of centuries were woven around the gigantic figure of their first leader and the founder of their religion and that have both hallowed and obscured that figure. Some fragments of sound tradition which had found no place in the Pentateuch may lie scattered in that material. One of these legends describes in an attractive fashion how the ambition of the man Moses had already displayed itself in his childhood. When Pharaoh took him into his arms and

playfully tossed him high, the little three-year-old
snatched the crown from Pharaoh's head and placed it
on his own. The king was startled at this omen and
took care to consult his sages.[1] Then, again, we are
told of victorious battles he fought as an Egyptian
captain in Ethiopia and, in the same connection, that
he fled the country because he had reason to fear the
envy of a faction at court or even of Pharaoh himself.
The Biblical story itself lends Moses certain features
in which one is inclined to believe. It describes him
as choleric, hot-tempered—as when in his indignation
he kills the brutal overseer who ill-treated a Jewish
workman, or when in his resentment at the defection
of his people he smashes the tables he has been given
on Mount Sinai. Indeed, God himself punished him
at long last for a deed of impatience—we are not told
what it was. Since such a trait does not lend itself to
glorification, it may very well be historical truth. Nor
can we reject even the possibility that many character
traits the Jews incorporated into their early conception of God when they made him jealous, stern, and
implacable were taken essentially from their memory
of Moses, for in truth it was not an invisible god, but
the man Moses, who had led them out of Egypt.

Another trait imputed to him deserves our special interest. Moses was said to have been "slow of
speech"—that is to say, he must have had a speech
impediment or inhibition—so that he had to call on
Aaron (who is called his brother) for assistance in his
supposed discussions with Pharaoh. This again may

[1] The same anecdote, slightly altered, is to be found in
Josephus.

be historical truth and would serve as a welcome addition to the endeavour to make the picture of this great man live. It may, however, have another and more important significance. The report may, in a slightly distorted way, recall the fact that Moses spoke another language and was not able to communicate with his Semitic Neo-Egyptians without the help of an interpreter—at least not at the beginning of their intercourse. Thus a fresh confirmation of the thesis: Moses was an Egyptian.

It looks now as if the train of thought has come to an end, at least for the time being. From the surmise that Moses was an Egyptian, be it proved or not, nothing more can be deduced for the moment. No historian can regard the Biblical account of Moses and the Exodus as other than a pious myth, which transformed a remote tradition in the interest of its own tendencies. How the tradition ran originally we do not know. What the distorting tendencies were we should like to guess, but we are kept in the dark by our ignorance of the historical events. That our reconstruction leaves no room for so many spectacular features of the Biblical text—the ten plagues, the passage through the Red Sea, the solemn law-giving on Mount Sinai—will not lead us astray. But we cannot remain indifferent on finding ourselves in opposition to the sober historical researches of our time.

These modern historians, well represented by Eduard Meyer,[1] follow the Biblical text in one decisive point. They concur that the Jewish tribes, who

[1] E. Meyer: *Die Israeliten und ihre Nachbarstämme* (1906).

later on became the people of Israel, at a certain time accepted a new religion. But this event did not take place in Egypt nor at the foot of a mount in the Sinai peninsula, but in a place called Meribat-Qadeš, an oasis distinguished by its abundance of springs and wells in the country south of Palestine between the eastern end of the Sinai peninsula and the western end of Arabia. There they took over the worship of a god Jahve, probably from the Arabic tribe of Midianites who lived near by. Presumably other neighbouring tribes were also followers of that God.

Jahve was certainly a volcano-god. As we know, however, Egypt has no volcanoes and the mountains of the Sinai peninsula have never been volcanic; on the other hand, volcanoes which may have been active up to a late period are found along the western border of Arabia. One of these mountains must have been the Sinai-Horeb which was believed to be Jahve's abode.[1] In spite of all the transformations the Biblical text has suffered, we are able to reconstruct—according to Meyer—the original character of the God: he is an uncanny, bloodthirsty demon who walks by night and shuns the light of day.[2]

The mediator between the people and the God at this birth of a new religion was called Moses. He was the son-in-law of the Midianite priest Jethro and was tending his flocks when he received the divine summons. Jethro visited him in Qadeš to give him instructions.

[1] The Biblical text retains certain passages telling us that Jahve descended from Sinai to Meribat-Qadeš.
[2] Op. cit., pp. 38, 58.

Eduard Meyer says, it is true, that he never doubted there was a kernel of historical truth in the story of the bondage in Egypt and the catastrophe of the Egyptians,[1] but evidently he does not know where that recognized fact belongs and what to do with it. Only the custom of circumcision is he willing to derive from the Egyptians. He enriches our earlier discussion by two important suggestions: first, that Joshua asked the people to accept circumcision "to roll away the reproach of Egypt"; and, secondly, by the quotation from Herodotus that the Phœnicians (which probably means the Jews) and the Syrians in Palestine themselves admitted having learned the custom of circumcision from the Egyptians.[2] But an Egyptian Moses does not appeal to him. "The Moses we know was the ancestor of the priests of Qadeš; he stood therefore in relation to the cult, was a figure of the genealogical myth and not a historical person." So not one of those who have treated him as a historical person (except those who accept tradition wholesale as historical truth) has succeeded in filling this empty shape with any content, in describing him as a concrete personality; they have had nothing to tell us about what he achieved or about his mission in history.[3]

On the other hand, Meyer never wearies of telling us about Moses' relation to Qadeš and Midian. "The figure of Moses so closely bound up with Midian and the holy places in the desert. . . ."[4] "This figure of Moses is inextricably associated with

[1] Ibid., p. 49.
[2] Ibid., p. 449.
[3] Ibid., p. 451.
[4] Ibid., p. 49.

Qadeš (Massa and Meriba); the relationship with a Midianite priest by marriage completes the picture. The connection with the Exodus, on the other hand, and the story of his youth in its entirety, are absolutely secondary and are merely the consequence of Moses' having to fit into a connected, continuous story." [1] He also observes that all the characteristics contained in the story of Moses' youth were later omitted. "Moses in Midian is no longer an Egyptian and Pharaoh's grandson, but a shepherd to whom Jahve reveals himself. In the story of the ten plagues his former relationships are no longer mentioned, although they could have been used very effectively, and the order to kill the Israelite first-born is entirely forgotten. In the Exodus and the perishing of the Egyptians Moses has no part at all; he is not even mentioned. The characteristics of a hero, which the childhood story presupposes, are entirely absent in the later Moses; he is only the man of God, a performer of miracles, provided with supernatural powers by Jahve." [2]

We cannot escape the impression that this Moses of Qadeš and Midian, to whom tradition could even ascribe the erection of a brazen serpent as a healing god, is quite a different person from the august Egyptian we had deduced, who disclosed to his people a religion in which all magic and sorcery were most strictly abhorred. Our Egyptian Moses differs perhaps no less from the Midian Moses than the universal god Aton differed from the demon Jahve on his

---

[1] Ibid., p. 72.
[2] Ibid., p. 47.

divine mountain. And if we concede any measure of truth to the information furnished by modern historians, then we have to admit that the thread we wished to draw from the surmise that Moses was an Egyptian has broken off for the second time; this time, so it seems, without any hope of its being tied again.

V

A way unexpectedly presents itself, however, out of this difficulty too. The efforts to recognize in Moses a figure transcending the priest of Qadeš, and confirming the renown with which tradition had invested him, were continued after Meyer by Gressmann and others. In 1922 Ernst Sellin made a discovery of decisive importance.[1] He found in the book of the Prophet Hosea (second half of the eighth century) unmistakable traces of a tradition to the effect that the founder of their religion, Moses, met a violent end in a rebellion of his stubborn and refractory people. The religion he had instituted was at the same time abandoned. This tradition is not restricted to Hosea; it recurs in the writings of most of the later Prophets; indeed, according to Sellin, it was the basis of all the later expectations of the Messiah. Towards the end of the Babylonian exile the hope arose among the Jewish people that the man they had so callously murdered would return from the realm of the dead and lead his contrite people—and perhaps not only his

---

[1] Ernst Sellin: *Mose und seine Bedeutung für die israelitisch-jüdische Religionsgeschichte* (1922).

people—into the land of eternal bliss. The palpable connections with the destiny of the Founder of a later religion do not lie in our present course.

Naturally, I am not in a position to decide whether Sellin has correctly interpreted the relevant passages in the Prophets. If he is right, however, we may regard as historically credible the tradition he recognized; for such things are not readily invented— there is no tangible motive for doing so. And if they have really happened, the wish to forget them is easily understood. We need not accept every detail of the tradition. Sellin thinks that Shittim in the land east of the Jordan is indicated as the scene of the violent deed. We shall see, however, that the choice of this locality does not accord with our argument.

Let us adopt from Sellin the surmise that the Egyptian Moses was killed by the Jews, and the religion he instituted abandoned. It allows us to spin our thread further without contradicting the trustworthy results of historical research. But we venture to be independent of the historians in other respects and to blaze our own trail. The Exodus from Egypt remains our starting-point. It must have been a considerable number that left the country with Moses; a small crowd would not have been worth the while of that ambitious man, with his great schemes. The immigrants had probably been in the country long enough to develop into a numerous people. We shall certainly not go astray, however, if we suppose with the majority of research workers that only a part of those who later became the Jewish people had undergone the fate of bondage in Egypt. In other words, the tribe returning from Egypt combined later in the country between Egypt and Canaan with other related tribes that had been settled there for some time. This union, from which was born the people of Israel, expressed itself in the adoption of a new religion, common to all the tribes, the religion of Jahve; according to Meyer, this came about in Qadeš under the influence of the Midianites. Thereupon the people felt strong enough to undertake the invasion of Canaan. It does not fit in with this course of events that the catastrophe to Moses and his religion should have taken place in the land east of the Jordan—it must have happened a long time before the union.

It is certain that many very diverse elements contributed to the building up of the Jewish people, but the greatest difference among them must have depended on whether they had experienced the sojourn in Egypt and what followed it, or not. From this point of view we may say that the nation was made up by the union of two constituents, and it accords with this fact that, after a short period of political unity, it broke asunder into two parts—the Kingdom of Israel and the Kingdom of Judah. History loves such restorations, in which later fusions are redissolved and former separations become once more apparent. The most impressive example—a very well-known one—was provided by the Reformation, when, after an interval of more than a thousand years, it brought to light again the frontier between the Germania that had been Roman and the part that had always remained independent. With the Jewish people we cannot verify such a faithful reproduction of the former state of affairs. Our knowledge of those times is too uncertain to permit the assumption that the northern Kingdom had absorbed the original settlers, the southern those returning from Egypt; but the later dissolution, in this case also, could not have been unconnected with the earlier union. The former Egyptians were probably fewer than the others, but they proved to be on a higher level culturally. They exercised a more important influence on the later development of the people because they brought with them a tradition the others lacked.

Perhaps they brought something else, something more tangible than a tradition. Among the greatest riddles of Jewish prehistoric times is that concerning the antecedents of the Levites. They are said to have been derived from one of the twelve tribes of Israel, the tribe of Levi, but no tradition has ever ventured to pronounce on where that tribe originally dwelt or what portion of the conquered country of Canaan had been allotted to it. They occupied the most important priestly positions, but yet they were distinguished from the priests. A Levite is not necessarily a priest; it is not the name of a caste. Our supposition about the person of Moses suggests an explanation. It is not credible that a great gentleman like the Egyptian Moses approached a people strange to him without an escort. He must have brought his retinue with him, his nearest adherents, his scribes, his servants. These were the original Levites. Tradition maintains that Moses was a Levite. This seems a transparent distortion of the actual state of affairs: the Levites were Moses' people. This solution is supported by what I mentioned in my previous essay: that in later times we find Egyptian names only among the Levites.[1] We may suppose that a fair number of these Moses people escaped the fate that overtook him and his religion. They increased in the following generations and fused with the people among whom they lived, but they remained faithful to their master, honoured his memory, and retained the tradition of his teaching. At the time of the union with the followers of Jahve they formed an influential minority, culturally superior to the rest.

I suggest—and it is only a suggestion so far—that between the downfall of Moses and the founding of a religion at Qadeš two generations were born and vanished, that perhaps even a century elapsed. I do not see my way to determine whether the Neo-Egyptians, as I should like to call those who returned from Egypt in distinction to the other Jews, met with their blood relations after these had already accepted the Jahve religion or before that had happened. Perhaps the latter is more likely. It makes no difference to the final result. What happened at Qadeš was a compromise, in which the part taken by the Moses tribe is unmistakable.

Here we may call again on the custom of circumcision, which—a kind of *"Leitfossil"*—has repeatedly rendered us important services. This custom also became the law in the Jahve religion, and—since it is inextricably connected with Egypt—its adoption

[1] This assumption fits in well with what Yahuda says about the Egyptian influence on early Jewish writings. See A. S. Yahuda: *Die Sprache des Pentateuch in ihren Beziehungen zum Ägyptischen* (1929).

must signify a concession to the people of Moses. They—or the Levites among them—would not forgo this sign of their consecration. They wanted to save so much of their old religion, and for that price they were willing to recognize the new deity and all that the Midian priests had to say about him. Possibly they managed to obtain still other concessions. I have already mentioned that Jewish ritual ordains a certain economy in the use of the name of God. Instead of Jahve they had to say Adonai. It is tempting to fit this commandment into our argument, but that is merely a surmise. The prohibition upon uttering the name of God is, as is well known, a primeval taboo. Why exactly it was renewed in the Jewish commandments is not quite clear; it is not out of the question that this happened under the influence of a new motive. There is no reason to suppose that the commandment was consistently followed; the word Jahve was freely used in the formation of personal theophorous names— that is, in combinations such as Jochanan, Jehu, Joshua. Yet there is something peculiar about this name. It is well known that Biblical exegesis recognizes two sources of the Hexateuch. They are called J and E because the one uses the holy name of Jahve, the other that of Elohim; Elohim, it is true, not Adonai. But we may here quote the remark of one writer: "The different names are a distinct sign of originally different gods." [1]

We admitted the adherence to the custom of circumcision as evidence that at the founding of the

[1] Hugo Gressmann: *Mose und seine Zeit* (Göttingen, 1913), p. 54.

new religion at Qadeš a compromise had taken place. What it consisted in we learn from both J and E; the two accounts coincide and must therefore go back to a common source, either a written source or an oral tradition. The guiding purpose was to prove the greatness and power of the new god Jahve. Since the Moses people attached such great importance to their experience of the Exodus from Egypt, the deed of freeing them had to be ascribed to Jahve; it had to be adorned with features that proved the terrific grandeur of this volcano-god, such as, for example, the pillar of smoke which changed to one of fire by night, or the storm that parted the waters so that the pursuers were drowned by the returning floods of water. The Exodus and the founding of the new religion were thus brought close together in time, the long interval between them being denied. The bestowal of the Ten Commandments too was said to have taken place, not at Qadeš, but at the foot of the holy mountain amid the signs of a volcanic eruption. This description, however, did a serious wrong to the memory of the man Moses; it was he, and not the volcano-god, who had freed his people from Egypt. Some compensation was therefore due to him, and it was given by transposing Moses to Qadeš or to the mount Sinai-Horeb and putting him in the place of the Midianite priest. We shall consider later how this solution satisfied another, irresistibly urgent tendency. By its means a balance, so to speak, was established: Jahve was allowed to extend his reach to Egypt from his mountain in Midia, while the existence and activity of Moses were transferred to Qadeš and the country east of the Jordan. This is how he became one with the person who later established a religion, the son-in-law of the Midianite Jethro, the man to whom he lent his name Moses. We know nothing personal, however, about this other Moses—he is entirely obscured by the first, the Egyptian Moses—except possibly from clues provided by the contradictions to be found in the Bible in the characterization of Moses. He is often enough described as masterful, hot-tempered, even violent, and yet it is also said of him that he was the most patient and "meek" of all men. It is clear that the latter qualities would have been of no use to the Egyptian Moses who planned such great and difficult projects for his people. Perhaps they belonged to the other, the Midianite. I think we are justified in separating the two persons from each other and in assuming that the Egyptian Moses never was in Qadeš and had never heard the name of Jahve, whereas the Midianite Moses never set foot in Egypt and knew nothing of Aton. In order to make the two people into one, tradition or legend had to bring the Egyptian Moses to Midian; and we have seen that more than one explanation was given for it.

VI

I am quite prepared to hear anew the reproach that I have put forward my reconstruction of the early history of the tribe of Israel with undue and unjustified certitude. I shall not feel this criticism to be too harsh, since it finds an echo in my own judgment. I know myself that this reconstruction has its weak places, but it also has its strong ones. On the whole the arguments in favour of continuing this work in the same direction prevail. The Biblical record before us contains valuable—nay, invaluable—historical evidence. It has, however, been distorted by tendentious influences and elaborated by the products of poetical invention. In our work we have already been able to divine one of these distorting tendencies. This discovery shall guide us on our way. It is a hint to uncover other similar distorting influences. If we find reasons for recognizing the distortions produced by them, then we shall be able to bring to light more of the true course of events.

Let us begin by marking what critical research work on the Bible has to say about how the Hexateuch—the five Books of Moses and the Book of Joshua, for they alone are of interest to us here—came to be written.[1] The oldest source is considered to be J, the Jahvistic, in the author of which the most modern research workers think they can recognize the priest Ebjatar, a contemporary of King David.[2] A little later, it is not known how much later, comes the so-called Elohistic, belonging to the northern Kingdom.[3] After the destruction of this Kingdom, in 722 B.C., a Jewish priest combined portions of J and E and added his own contributions. His compilation is designated as JE. In the seventh century Deuteron-

[1] *Encyclopædia Britannica* (eleventh edition, 1910), article: "Bible."
[2] See Auerbach: *Wüste und Gelobtes Land* (1932).
[3] Astruc in 1753 was the first to distinguish between Jahvist and Elohist.

omy, the fifth book, was added, it being alleged that the whole of it had been newly found in the Temple. In the time after the destruction of the Temple, in 586 B.C., during the Exile and after the return, is placed the rewriting called the Priestly Code. The fifth century saw a definitive revision, and since then the work has not been materially altered.[1]

The history of King David and his time is most probably the work of one of his contemporaries. It is real history, five hundred years before Herodotus, the "Father of History." One would begin to understand this achievement if one assumed, in terms of my hypothesis, Egyptian influence. The suggestion has even been made[2] that early Israelites, the scribes of Moses, had a hand in the invention of the first alphabet.[3] How far the accounts of former times are based on earlier sources or on oral tradition, and what interval elapsed between an event and its fixation by writing, we are naturally unable to know. The text, however,

[1] It is historically certain that the Jewish type was definitely fixed as a result of the reforms by Ezra and Nehemiah in the fifth century B.C., therefore after the Exile, during the reign of the friendly Persians. According to our reckoning, approximately nine hundred years had then passed since the appearance of Moses. By these reforms the regulations aiming at the consecration of the chosen people were taken seriously: the separation from the other tribes was put into force by forbidding mixed marriages; the Pentateuch, the real compilation of the law, was codified in its definitive form; the rewriting known as the Priestly Code was finished. It seems certain, however, that the reform did not adopt any new tendencies, but simply took over and consolidated former suggestions.

[2] Cf. Yahuda, op. cit., p. 142.

[3] If they were bound by the prohibition against making images they even had a motive for forsaking the hieroglyphic picture writing when they adapted their written signs for the expression of a new language.

as we find it today tells us enough about its own history. Two distinct forces, diametrically opposed to each other, have left their traces on it. On the one hand, certain transformations got to work on it, falsifying the text in accord with secret tendencies, maiming and extending it until it was turned into its opposite. On the other hand, an indulgent piety reigned over it, anxious to keep everything as it stood, indifferent to whether the details fitted together or nullified one another. Thus almost everywhere there can be found striking omissions, disturbing repetitions, palpable contradictions, signs of things the communication of which was never intended. The distortion of a text is not unlike a murder. The difficulty lies not in the execution of the deed but in the doing away with the traces. One could wish to give the word "distortion" the double meaning to which it has a right, although it is no longer used in this sense. It should mean not only "to change the appearance of," but also "to wrench apart," "to put in another place." That is why in so many textual distortions we may count on finding the suppressed and abnegated material hidden away somewhere, though in an altered shape and torn out of its original connection. Only it is not always easy to recognize it.

The distorting tendencies we want to detect must have influenced the traditions before they were written down. One of them, perhaps the strongest of all, we have already discovered. I said that when the new god Jahve in Qadeš was instituted, something had to be done to glorify him. It is truer to say he had to be established, made room for; traces of former religions had to be extinguished. This seems to have been done successfully with the religion of the settled tribes; no more was heard of it. With the returning tribes the task was not so easy; they were determined not to be deprived of the Exodus from Egypt, the man Moses, and the custom of circumcision. It is true they had been in Egypt, but they had left it again, and from now on, every trace of Egyptian influence was to be denied. Moses was disposed of by displacing him to Midian and Qadeš and making him into one person with the priest who founded the Jahve religion. Circumcision, the most compromising sign of the dependence on Egypt, had to be retained, but, in spite of all the existing evidence, every endeavour was made to divorce this custom from Egypt. The enigmatic passage in Exodus, written in an almost incomprehensible style, saying that God was wroth with Moses for neglecting circumcision and that his Midianite wife saved his life by a speedy operation can be interpreted only as a deliberate contradiction of the significant truth. We shall soon come across another invention for the purpose of invalidating a piece of inconvenient evidence.

It is hardly to be described as a new tendency— it is only the continuation of the same one—when we find an endeavour completely to deny that Jahve was a new god, one alien to the Jews. For that purpose the myths of the patriarchs, Abraham, Isaac, and Jacob, are drawn upon. Jahve maintains that he had been the God of those patriarchs; it is true—and he has to admit this himself—they did not worship him under this name.[1]

He does not add under what other name he used to be worshipped. Here the opportunity was taken to deal a decisive blow at the Egyptian origin of the custom of circumcision. Jahve was said to have already demanded it from Abraham, to have instituted it as a sign of the bond between him and Abraham's descendants. This, however, was a particularly clumsy invention. If one wished to use a sign to distinguish someone from other people, one would choose something that the others did not possess—certainly not something that millions could show. An Israelite, finding himself in Egypt, would have had to recognize all Egyptians as brothers, bound by the same bond, brothers in Jahve. The fact that circumcision was native to the Egyptians could not possibly have been unknown to the Israelites who created the text of the Bible. The passage from Joshua quoted by Eduard Meyer freely admits this, but nevertheless the fact had at all costs to be denied.

We cannot expect religious myths to pay scrupulous attention to logical connections. Otherwise the feeling of the people might have taken exception, justifiably, to the behaviour of a deity who makes a covenant with his patriarchs containing mutual obligations, and then ignores his human partners for centuries until it suddenly occurs to him to reveal himself again to their descendants. Still more astonishing

[1] The restrictions in the use of the new name do not become any more comprehensible through this. though much more suspect.

is the conception of a god suddenly "choosing" a people, making it "his" people and himself its own god. I believe it is the only case in the history of human religions. In other cases the people and their god belong inseparably together; they are one from the beginning. Sometimes, it is true, we hear of a people adopting another god, but never of a god choosing a new people. Perhaps we approach an understanding of this unique happening when we reflect on the connection between Moses and the Jewish people. Moses had stooped to the Jews, had made them his people; they were his "chosen people." [1]

[1] Jahve was undoubtedly a volcano-god. There was no reason for the inhabitants of Egypt to worship him. I am certainly not the first to be struck by the similarity of the name Jahve to the root of the name of another god: Jupiter, Jovis. The composite name Jochanaan, made up in part from the Hebrew word Jahve and having a rather similar meaning to that of Godfrey or its Punic equivalent Hannibal, has become one of the most popular names of European Christendom in the forms of Johann, John, Jean, Juan. When the Italians reproduce it in the shape of Giovanni and then call one day of the week Giovedi they bring to light again a similarity which perhaps means nothing or possibly means very much. Far-reaching possibilities, though very insecure ones, open out here. In those dark centuries which historical research is only beginning to explore, the countries around the eastern basin of the Mediterranean were apparently the scene of frequent and violent volcanic eruptions, which were bound to make the deepest impression on the inhabitants. Evans supposes that the final destruction of the palace of Minos at Knossos was also the result of an earthquake. In Crete, as probably everywhere in the Ægean world, the great mother goddess was then worshipped. The observation that she was unable to guard her house against the attack of a stronger power might have contributed to her having to cede her place to a male deity, whereupon the volcano-god had the first right to replace her. Zeus still bears the name of "the Earth-shaker." There is hardly a doubt that in those obscure times mother deities were replaced by male gods (perhaps originally their sons). Especially impressive is the fate of

There was yet another purpose in bringing the patriarchs into the new Jahve religion. They had lived in Canaan; their memory was connected with certain localities in the country. Possibly they themselves had been Canaanite heroes or local divinities whom the immigrating Israelites had adopted for their early history. By evoking them one gave proof, so to speak, of having been born and bred in the country, and denied the odium that clings to the alien conqueror. It was a clever turn: the god Jahve gave them only what their ancestors had once possessed.

In the later contributions to the Biblical text the tendency to avoid mentioning Qadeš met with success. The site of the founding of the new religion definitely became the divine mountain Sinai-Horeb. The motive is not clearly visible; perhaps they did not want to be reminded of the influence of Midian. But all later distortions, especially those of the Priestly Code, serve another aim. There was no longer any need to alter in a particular direction descriptions of happenings of long ago; that had long been done. On the other hand, an endeavour was made to date back to an early time certain laws and institutions of the present, to base them as a rule on the Mosaic law, and to derive from this their claim to holiness and binding force. However much the picture of past times in this way became falsified, the procedure does not lack a certain psychological justification. It reflected the fact that in the course of many centuries—

Pallas Athene, who was no doubt the local form of the mother deity; through the religious revolution she was reduced to a daughter, robbed of her own mother, and eternally debarred from motherhood by the taboo of virginity.

about eight hundred years had elapsed between the
Exodus and the fixation of the Biblical text by Ezra
and Nehemiah—the religion of Jahve had followed a
retrograde development that had culminated in a
fusion (perhaps to the point of actual identity) with
the original religion of Moses.

And this is the essential outcome: the fateful
content of the religious history of the Jews.

VII

Among all the events of Jewish prehistory that
poets, priests, and historians of a later age undertook
to portray, there was an outstanding one the suppression of which was called for by the most obvious and
best of human motives. It was the murder of the great
leader and liberator Moses, which Sellin divined from
clues furnished by the Prophets. Sellin's presumption
cannot be called fanciful; it is probable enough.
Moses, trained in Ikhnaton's school, employed the
same methods as the king; he gave commands and
forced his religion on the people.[1] Perhaps Moses' doctrine was still more uncompromising than that of his
master; he had no need to retain any connection with
the religion of the sun-god since the school of On
would have no importance for his alien people. Moses
met with the same fate as Ikhnaton, the fate that
awaits all enlightened despots. The Jewish people of
Moses were quite as unable to bear such a highly

[1] In those times any other form of influence would
scarcely have been possible.

spiritualized religion, to find in what it offered satisfaction for their needs, as were the Egyptians of the Eighteenth Dynasty. In both cases the same thing happened: those who felt themselves kept in tutelage, or who felt dispossessed, revolted and threw off the burden of a religion that had been forced on them. But while the tame Egyptians waited until fate had removed the sacred person of their Pharaoh, the savage Semites took their destiny into their own hands and did away with their tyrant.[1]

Nor can we maintain that the Biblical text preserved to us does not prepare us for such an end to Moses. The account of the "wandering in the wilderness"—which might stand for the time of Moses' rule—describes a series of grave revolts against his authority which, by Jahve's command, were suppressed with savage chastisement. It is easy to imagine that one of those revolts came to another end than the text admits. The people's falling away from the new religion is also mentioned in the text, though as a mere episode. It is the story of the golden calf, where by an adroit turn the breaking of the tables of the law—which has to be understood symbolically (= "he has broken the law")—is ascribed to Moses himself and imputed to his angry indignation.

There came a time when the people regretted the murder of Moses and tried to forget it. This was

---

[1] It is truly remarkable how seldom during the millennia of Egyptian history we hear of violent depositions or assassinations of a Pharaoh. A comparison with Assyrian history, for example, must increase this astonishment. The reason may, of course, be that with the Egyptians historical recording served exclusively official purposes.

certainly so at the time of the coming together at Qadeš. If, however, the Exodus were brought nearer in time to the founding of their religion in the oasis, and one allowed Moses, instead of the other founder, to help in it, then not only were the claims of the Moses people satisfied, but the painful fact of his violent removal was also successfully denied. In reality it is most unlikely that Moses could have participated in the events at Qadeš, even if his life had not been shortened.

Here we must try to elucidate the sequence of these events. I have placed the Exodus from Egypt in the time after the extinction of the Eighteenth Dynasty (1350 B.C.). It might have happened then or a little later, for the Egyptian chroniclers included the subsequent years of anarchy in the reign of Haremhab, the king who brought it to an end and who reigned until 1315 B.C. The next aid in fixing the chronology—and it is the only one—is given by the stele of Merneptah (1225–1215 B.C.), which extols the victory over Isiraal (Israel) and the destruction of their seeds (*sic*). Unfortunately the value of this stele is doubtful; it is taken to be evidence that Israelite tribes were at that date already settled in Canaan.[1] Meyer rightly concludes from this stele that Merneptah could not have been the Pharaoh of the Exodus, as had previously been assumed. The Exodus must belong to an earlier period. The question of who was Pharaoh at the time of the Exodus appears to me an idle one. There was no Pharaoh at that time, because the Exodus happened during the interregnum. But

[1] Meyer, op. cit., p. 222.

the Merneptah stele does not throw any light on the possible date of the fusion and the acceptance of the new religion in Qadeš. All we can say with certainty is that they took place at some time between 1350 and 1215. Within this century let us assume the Exodus to have been very near to the first date, the events in Qadeš not far from the second. The greater part of the period we would reserve for the interval between the two events. A fairly long time would be necessary for the passions of the returning tribes to cool down after the murder of Moses and for the influence of the Moses people, the Levites, to have become as strong as the compromise in Qadeš presupposes. Two generations, sixty years, might suffice, but only just. The date inferred from the stele of Merneptah falls too early, and as we know that in our hypothesis one assumption only rests on another, we have to admit that this discussion shows a weak spot in the construction. Unfortunately everything connected with the settling of the Jewish people in Canaan is highly obscure and confused. We might, of course, use the expedient of supposing that the name in the Israel stele does not refer to the tribes whose fate we are trying to follow and who later on were united in the people of Israel. After all, the name of the Habiru (= Hebrews) from the Amarna time was also passed on to this people.

Whenever it was that the different tribes were united into a nation by accepting the same religion, it might very well have been an occurrence of no great importance for the history of the world. The

new religion might have been swept away by the
stream of events, Jahve would then have taken his
place in the procession of erstwhile gods which Flau-
bert visualized, and of his people all the twelve tribes
would have been "lost," not only the ten for whom
the Anglo-Saxons have so long been searching. The
god Jahve, to whom the Midianite Moses led a new
people, was probably in no way a remarkable being.
A rude, narrow-minded local god, violent and bloodthirsty, he had promised his adherents to give them
"a land flowing with milk and honey" and he encour-
aged them to rid the country of its present inhabitants "with the edge of the sword." It is truly astonishing that in spite of all the revisions in the Biblical
text so much was allowed to stand whereby we may
recognize his original nature. It is not even sure that
his religion was a true monotheism, that it denied the
character of God to other divinities. It probably sufficed that one's own god was more powerful than all
strange gods. When the sequence of events took quite
another course than such beginnings would lead us
to expect, there can be only one reason for it. To one
part of the people the Egyptian Moses had given another and more spiritual conception of God, a single
God who embraces the whole world, one as all-loving
as he was all-powerful, who, averse to all ceremonial
and magic, set humanity as its highest aim a life of
truth and justice. For, incomplete as our information
about the ethical side of the Aton religion may be, it
is surely significant that Ikhnaton regularly described
himself in his inscriptions as "living in Maat" (truth,

justice).[1] In the long run it did not matter that the people, probably after a very short time, renounced the teaching of Moses and removed the man himself. The tradition itself remained and its influence reached—though only slowly, in the course of centuries—the aim that was denied to Moses himself. The god Jahve attained undeserved honour when, from Qadeš onward, Moses' deed of liberation was put down to his account; but he had to pay dear for this usurpation. The shadow of the god whose place he had taken became stronger than himself; at the end of the historical development there arose beyond his being that of the forgotten Mosaic god. None can doubt that it was only the idea of this other god that enabled the people of Israel to surmount all their hardships and to survive until our time.

It is no longer possible to determine the part the Levites played in the final victory of the Mosaic god over Jahve. When the compromise at Qadeš was effected they had raised their voice for Moses, their memory being still green of the master whose followers and countrymen they were. During the centuries since then the Levites had become one with the people or with the priesthood and it had become the main task of the priests to develop and supervise the ritual, besides caring for the holy texts and revising them in accordance with their purposes. But was not all this sacrifice and ceremonial at bottom only magic and black art, such as the old doctrine of Moses had

---

[1] His hymns lay stress not only on the universality and oneness of God, but also on his loving-kindness for all creatures; they invite believers to enjoy nature and its beauties. Cf. Breasted: *The Dawn of Conscience*.

unconditionally condemned? There arose from the midst of the people an unending succession of men, not necessarily descended from Moses' people, but seized by the great and powerful tradition which had gradually grown in darkness, and it was these men, the Prophets, who sedulously preached the old Mosaic doctrine: the Deity spurns sacrifice and ceremonial; he demands only belief and a life of truth and justice (Maat). The efforts of the Prophets met with enduring success; the doctrines with which they re-established the old belief became the permanent content of the Jewish religion. It is honour enough for the Jewish people that it has kept alive such a tradition and produced men who lent it their voice, even if the stimulus had first come from outside, from a great stranger.

    This description of events would leave me with a feeling of uncertainty were it not that I can refer to the judgment of other, expert research workers who see the importance of Moses for the history of Jewish religion in the same light, although they do not recognize his Egyptian origin. Sellin says, for example:[1] "Therefore we have to picture the true religion of Moses, the belief he proclaimed in one ethical god, as being from now on, as a matter of course, the possession of a small circle within the people. We cannot expect to find it from the start in the official cult, in the priests' religion, in the general belief of the people. All we can expect is that here and there a spark flies up from the spiritual fire he had kindled, that his ideas have not died out, but have quietly influenced

[1] Sellin, op. cit., p. 52.

beliefs and customs until, sooner or later, under the
influence of special events, or through some personality particularly immersed in this belief, they broke
forth again more strongly and gained dominance with
the broad mass of the people. It is from this point of
view that we have to regard the early religious history
of the old Israelites. Were we to reconstruct the Mosaic religion after the pattern laid down in the historical documents that describe the religion of the
first five centuries in Canaan, we should fall into the
worst methodical error." Volz[1] expresses himself still
more explicitly. He says that "the heaven-soaring work
of Moses was at first hardly understood and feebly
carried out, until during the course of centuries it
penetrated more and more into the spirit of the people and at last found kindred souls in the great prophets who continued the work of the lonely founder."

With this I have come to an end, my sole purpose having been to fit the figure of an Egyptian
Moses into the framework of Jewish history. I may
now express my conclusion in the shortest formula:
To the well-known *duality* of that history—*two peoples* who fuse together to form one nation, *two king-
doms* into which this nation divides, *two names* for
the Deity in the source of the Bible—we add two new
ones: the founding of *two* new religions, the first one
ousted by the second and yet reappearing victorious,
two founders of religion, who are both called by the
same name, Moses, and whose personalities we have to
separate from each other. And all these dualities are
necessary consequences of the first: one section of the

[1] Paul Volz: *Mose* (Tübingen, 1907), p. 64.

people passed through what may properly be termed a traumatic experience which the other was spared. There still remains much to discuss, to explain, and to assert. Only then would the interest in our purely historical study be fully warranted. In what exactly consists the intrinsic nature of a tradition, and in what resides its peculiar power, how impossible it is to deny the personal influence of individual great men on the history of the world, what profanation of the grandiose multiformity of human life we commit if we recognize as sole motives those springing from material needs, from what sources certain ideas, especially religious ones, derive the power with which they subjugate individuals and peoples—to study all this in the particular case of Jewish history would be an alluring task. Such a continuation of my essay would link up with conclusions laid down twenty-five years ago in *Totem and Taboo*. But I hardly trust my powers any further.

Part III. Moses, His People, and Monotheistic Religion

Prefatory Notes

1. Written before March 1938 (Vienna)

With the audacity of one who has little or nothing to lose I propose to break a well-founded resolution for the second time and to follow up my two essays on Moses (*Imago*, Bd. XXIII, Heft 1 and 3) with the final part, till now withheld. When I finished the last essay I said I knew full well that my powers would not suffice for the task. I was, of course, referring to the weakening of the creative faculties which accompanies old age,[1] but there was also another obstacle. We live in very remarkable times. We find with astonishment that progress has concluded an

[1] I do not share the opinion of my gifted contemporary Bernard Shaw that men would achieve anything worth while only if they could attain the age of three hundred years. With the mere lengthening of the period of life nothing would be gained unless much in the conditions of life were radically changed as well.

alliance with barbarism. In Soviet Russia the attempt has been made to better the life of a hundred million people till now held in suppression. The authorities were bold enough to deprive them of the anodyne of religion and wise enough to grant them a reasonable measure of sexual freedom. But in doing so they subjected them to the most cruel coercion and robbed them of every possibility of freedom of thought. With similar brutality the Italian people are being educated to order and a sense of duty. It was a real weight off the heart to find, in the case of the German people, that retrogression into all but prehistoric barbarism can come to pass independently of any progressive idea. Be that as it may, events have taken such a course that today the conservative democracies have become the guardians of cultural progress and that, strangely enough, just the institution of the Catholic Church has put up a sturdy resistance against the danger to culture. The Catholic Church. which so far has been the implacable enemy of all freedom of thought and has resolutely opposed any idea of this world being governed by advance towards the recognition of truth!

We are living here in a Catholic country under the protection of that Church, uncertain how long the protection will last. So long as it does last I naturally hesitate to do anything that is bound to awaken the hostility of that Church. It is not cowardice. but caution; the new enemy[1]—and I shall guard against doing anything that would serve his interests—is more dangerous than the old one, with whom we have

[1] i.e., German National Socialism.—*Translator*.

learned to live in peace. Psychoanalytic research is in any case the subject of suspicious attention from Catholicism. I do not maintain that this suspicion is unmerited. If our research leads us to a result that reduces religion to the status of a neurosis of mankind and explains its grandiose powers in the same way as we should a neurotic obsession in our individual patients, then we may be sure we shall incur in this country the greatest resentment of the powers that be. It is not that I have anything new to say, nothing that I did not clearly express a quarter of a century ago. All that, however, has been forgotten, and it would undoubtedly have some effect were I to repeat it now and to illustrate it by an example typical of the way in which religions are founded. It would probably lead to our being forbidden to work in psychoanalysis. Such violent methods of suppression are by no means alien to the Catholic Church; she feels it rather as an intrusion into her privileges when other people resort to the same means. Psychoanalysis, however, which has travelled everywhere during the course of my long life, has not yet found a more serviceable home than in the city where it was born and grew.

I do not only think so, I know that this external danger will deter me from publishing the last part of my treatise on Moses. I have tried to remove this obstacle by telling myself that my fear is based on an overestimation of my personal importance, and that the authorities would probably be quite indifferent to what I should have to say about Moses and the origin of monotheistic religions. Yet I do not feel sure that my judgment is correct. It seems to me more likely that malice and an appetite for sensation would make up for the importance I may lack in the eyes of the world. So I shall not publish this essay. But that need not hinder me from writing it. The more so since it was written once before, two years ago, and thus only needs rewriting and adding to the two previous essays. Thus it may lie hid until the time comes when it may safely venture into the light of day, or until someone else who reaches the same opinions and conclusions can be told: "In darker days there lived a man who thought as you did."

II. *June 1938* (*London*)

The exceptionally great difficulties which have weighed on me during the composition of this essay dealing with Moses—inner misgivings as well as external hindrances—are the reason why this third and final part comes to have two different prefaces which contradict—indeed, even cancel—each other. For in the short interval between writing the two prefaces the outer conditions of the author have radically changed. Formerly I lived under the protection of the Catholic Church and feared that by publishing the essay I should lose that protection and that the practitioners and students of psychoanalysis in Austria would be forbidden their work. Then, suddenly, the German invasion broke in on us and Catholicism proved to be, as the Bible has it, but "a broken reed." In the certainty of persecution—now not only because of my work, but also because of my "race"—I left, with many friends, the city which from early childhood, through seventy-eight years, had been a home to me.

I found the kindliest welcome in beautiful, free, generous England. Here I live now, a welcome guest, relieved from that oppression and happy that I may again speak and write—I almost said "think"—as I want or have to. I dare now to make public the last part of my essay.

There are no more external hindrances or at least none that need alarm one. In the few weeks of my stay I have received a large number of greetings, from friends who told me how glad they were to see me here, and from people unknown to me, barely interested in my work, who simply expressed their satisfaction that I had found freedom and security here. Besides all this there came, with a frequency bewildering to a foreigner, letters of another kind, expressing concern for the weal of my soul and anxious to point me the way to Christ and to enlighten me about the future of Israel. The good people who wrote thus could not have known much about me. I expect, however, that when this new work of mine becomes known among my new compatriots I shall lose with my correspondents and a number of the others something of the sympathy they now extend to me.

The inner difficulties were not to be changed by the different political system and the new domicile. Now as then I am uneasy when confronted with my own work; I miss the consciousness of unity and intimacy that should exist between the author and his work. This does not mean that I lack conviction in the correctness of my conclusions. That conviction I acquired a quarter of a century ago, when I wrote my book on *Totem and Taboo* (in 1912), and it has only become stronger since. From then on I have never doubted that religious phenomena are to be understood only on the model of the neurotic symptoms of the individual, which are so familiar to us, as a return of long-forgotten important happenings in the primeval history of the human family, that they owe their obsessive character to that very origin and therefore derive their effect on mankind from the historical truth they contain. My uncertainty begins only at the point when I ask myself the question whether I have succeeded in proving this for the example of Jewish monotheism chosen here. To my critical faculties this treatise, proceeding from a study of the man Moses, seems like a dancer balancing on one toe. If I had not been able to find support in the analytic interpretation of the exposure myth and pass thence to Sellin's suggestion concerning Moses' end, the whole treatise would have to remain unwritten. However, let me proceed.

I begin by abstracting the results of my second, purely historical, essay on Moses. I shall not examine them critically here, since they form the premises of the psychological discussions which are based on them and which continually revert to them.

Section I

1. The Historical Premisses

The historical background of the events which have aroused our interest is as follows: Through the conquests of the Eighteenth Dynasty Egypt had become a world empire. The new imperialism was reflected in the development of certain religious ideas, if not in those of the whole people, yet in those of the governing and intellectually active upper stratum. Under the influence of the priests of the sun-god at On (Heliopolis), possibly strengthened by suggestions from Asia, there arose the idea of a universal god, Aton—no longer restricted to one people and one country. With the young Amenhotep IV (who later changed his name to Ikhnaton) a Pharaoh succeeded to the throne who knew no higher interest than in developing the idea of such a god. He raised the Aton religion to the official religion and thereby the universal God became the *Only* God; all that was said of other gods became deceit and guile. With a superb implacability he resisted all the temptations of magical thought and discarded the illusion, dear particularly to the Egyptians, of a life after death. With an astonishing premonition of later scientific knowledge he recognized in the energy of the sun's radiation the source of all life on earth and worshipped the sun as the symbol of his God's power. He gloried in his joy in the Creation and in his life in Maat (truth and justice).

It is the first case in the history of mankind, and perhaps the purest, of a monotheistic religion. A deeper knowledge of the historical and psychological conditions of its origin would be of inestimable value. Care was taken, however, that not much information concerning the Aton religion should come down to us. Already under the reign of Ikhnaton's weak successors everything he had created broke down. The priesthood he had suppressed vented their fury on his memory. The Aton religion was abolished; the capital of the heretic Pharaoh demolished and pillaged. In 1350 B.C. the Eighteenth Dynasty was extinguished; after an interval of anarchy the general Haremhab, who reigned until 1315 B.C., restored order. Ikhnaton's reforms seemed to be but an episode, doomed to be forgotten.

This is what has been established historically, and at this point our work of hypothesis begins. Among the intimates of Ikhnaton was a man who was perhaps called Thothmes, as so many others were at that time;[1] the name does not matter, but its second part must have been "-mose." He held high rank and

[1] This, for example, was also the name of the sculptor whose workroom was discovered in Tell-el-Amarna.

was a convinced adherent of the Aton religion, but, in contradistinction to the brooding king, he was forceful and passionate. For this man the death of Ikhnaton and the abolishing of his religion meant the end of all his hopes. Only proscribed or recanting could he remain in Egypt. If he were governor of a border province he might well have come into touch with a certain Semitic tribe which had immigrated several generations before. In his disappointment and loneliness he turned to those strangers and sought in them for a compensation of what he had lost. He chose them for his people and tried to realize his own ideals through them. After he had left Egypt with them, accompanied by his immediate followers, he hallowed them by the custom of circumcision, gave them laws, and introduced them to the Aton religion, which the Egyptians had just discarded. Perhaps the rules the man Moses imposed on his Jews were even harder than those of his master and teacher Ikhnaton; perhaps he also relinquished the connection with the sun-god of On, to whom the latter had still adhered.

For the Exodus from Egypt we must fix the time of the interregnum after 1350 B.C. The subsequent periods of time until possession was taken of the land of Canaan are especially obscure. Out of the darkness which the Biblical text has here left—or rather created—the historical research of our days can distinguish two facts. The first, discovered by Ernst Sellin, is that the Jews, who even according to the Bible were stubborn and unruly towards their lawgiver and leader, rebelled at last, killed him, and threw off the imposed Aton religion as the Egyptians had done before them. The second fact, proved by Eduard Meyer, is that these Jews on their return from Egypt united with tribes nearly related to them, in the country bordering on Palestine, the Sinai peninsula, and Arabia, and that there, in a fertile spot called Qadeš, they accepted under the influence of the Arabian Midianites a new religion, the worship of the volcano-god Jahve. Soon after this they were ready to conquer Canaan.

The relationship in time of these two events to each other and to the Exodus is very uncertain. The next historical allusion is given in a stele of the Pharaoh Merneptah, who reigned until 1215 B.C., which numbers "Israel" among the vanquished in his conquests in Syria and Palestine. If we take the date of this stele as a *terminus ad quem,* there remains for the whole course of events, starting from the Exodus, about a century—after 1350 until before 1215. It is possible, however, that the name Israel does not yet refer to the tribes whose fate we are here following and that in reality we have a longer period at our disposal. The settling of the later Jewish people in Canaan was certainly not a swiftly achieved conquest; it was rather a series of successive struggles and must have stretched over a longish period. If we discard the restriction imposed by the Merneptah stele, we may more readily assume thirty years, a generation, as the the time of Moses,[1] and two generations at least, prob-

---

[1] This would accord with the forty years' wandering in the desert of which the Bible tells us.

ably more, until the union in Qadeš took place;[1] the
interval between Qadeš and the setting out for Canaan
need not have been long. Jewish tradition had—as I
have shown in my last essay—good reason to shorten
the interval between the Exodus and the foundation
of a religion in Qadeš; our argument would incline
us to favour the contrary.

Till now we have been concerned with the external aspects of the story, with an attempt to fill in
the gaps of our historical knowledge—in part a repetition of my second essay. Our interest follows the fate
of Moses and his doctrines, to which the revolt of
the Jews only apparently put an end. From the Jahvist
account—written down about 1000 B.C., though doubtless founded on earlier material—we have learned that
the union of the tribes and the foundation of a religion in Qadeš represented a compromise, the two
parts of which are still easily distinguishable. One
partner was concerned only in denying the recency
and foreignness of the God Jahve and in heightening
his claim to the people's devotion. The other partner
would not renounce memories, so dear to him, of the
liberation from Egypt and the magnificent figure of
his leader Moses; and, indeed, he succeeded in finding
a place for the fact as well as for the man in the new
representation of Jewish early history, in retaining at
least the outer sign of the Moses religion—namely, circumcision—and in insisting on certain restrictions in
the use of the new divine name. I have said that the

[1] Thus about 1350–40 to 1320–10 for Moses, 1260 or perhaps rather later for Qadeš, the Merneptah stele before 1215.

people who insisted on those demands were the descendants of the Moses followers, the Levites, separated by a few generations only from the actual contemporaries and compatriots of Moses and attached to his memory by a tradition still green. The poetically elaborated accounts attributed to the Jahvist and to his later competitor, the Elohist, are like gravestones, under which the truth about those early matters, about the nature of the Mosaic religion and the violent removal of the great man—truths withdrawn from the knowledge of later generations—should, so to speak, be laid to eternal rest. And if we have divined aright the course of events, there is nothing mysterious about them; it might very well, however, have been the definite end of the Moses episode in the history of the Jewish people.

The remarkable thing about it is that this was not so, that the most important effects of that experience should appear much later and should in the course of many centuries gradually force their way to expression. It is not likely that Jahve was very different in character from the gods of the neighbouring peoples and tribes; he wrestled with the other gods, it is true, just as the tribes fought among themselves, yet we may assume that a Jahve-worshipper of that time would never have dreamt of doubting the existence of the gods of Canaan, Moab, Amalek, and so on, any more than he would the existence of the people who believed in them. The monotheistic idea, which had blazed up in Ikhnaton's time, was again obscured and was to remain in darkness for a long time to come. On the island Elephantine, close to the first cataract of the Nile, discoveries have yielded the astonishing information that a Jewish military colony, settled there centuries ago, worshipped in their temples besides their chief god, Jahu, two female deities, one of whom was called Anat-Jahu. Those Jews, it is true, had been separated from the mother country and had not gone through the same religious development; the Persian government (in the fifth century B.C.) Communicated to them the new ceremonial regulations of Jerusalem.[1] Returning to earlier times, we may surely say that Jahve was quite unlike the Mosaic God. Aton had been a pacifist, like his deputy on earth—or rather his model—the Pharaoh Ikhnaton, who looked on with folded arms as the Empire his ancestors had won fell to pieces. For a people that was preparing to conquer new lands by violence Jahve was certainly better suited. Moreover, what was worthy of honour in the Mosaic God was beyond the comprehension of a primitive people.

I have already mentioned—and in this I am supported by the opinion of others—that the central fact of the development of Jewish religion was this: in the course of time Jahve lost his own character and became more and more like the old God of Moses, Aton. Differences remained, it is true, and at first sight they would seem important; yet they are easy to explain. Aton had begun his reign in Egypt in a happy period of security, and even when the Empire began to shake in its foundations, his followers had been able to turn away from worldly matters and to continue

[1] Auerbach: *Wüste und gelobtes Land,* Bd. II (1936).

praising and enjoying his creations. To the Jewish people fate dealt a series of severe trials and painful experiences, so their God became hard, relentless, and, as it were, wrapped in gloom. He retained the character of a universal God who reigned over all lands and peoples; the fact, however, that his worship had passed from the Egyptians to the Jews found its expression in the added doctrine that the Jews were his chosen people, whose special obligations would in the end find their special reward. It might not have been easy for that people to reconcile their belief in their being preferred to all others by an all-powerful God with the dire experiences of their sad fate. But they did not let doubts assail them, they increased their own feelings of guilt to silence their mistrust and perhaps in the end they referred to "God's unfathomable will," as religious people do to this day. It there was wonder that he allowed ever new tyrants to come who subjected and ill-treated his people—the Assyrians, Babylonians, Persians—yet his power was recognized in that all those wicked enemies were defeated in their turn and their empires destroyed.

In three important points the later Jewish God became identical with the old Mosaic God. The first and decisive point is that he was really recognized as the only God, beside whom another god was unthinkable. Ikhnaton's monotheism was taken seriously by an entire people; indeed, this people clung to it to such an extent that it became the principal content of their intellectual life and displaced all other interests. The people and the priesthood, now the dominating part of it, were unanimous on that point; but the priests, in confining their activities to elaborating the ceremonial for his worship, found themselves in opposition to strong tendencies within the people which endeavoured to revive two other doctrines of Moses about his God. The Prophets' voices untiringly proclaimed that God disdained ceremonial and sacrifice and asked nothing but a belief in him and a life in truth and justice. When they praised the simplicity and holiness of their life in the desert they surely stood under the influence of Mosaic ideals.

It is time now to raise the question whether there is any need at all to invoke Moses' influence on the final shape of the Jewish idea of their God, whether it is not enough to assume a spontaneous development to a higher spirituality during a cultural life extending over many centuries. On this possible explanation, which would put an end to all our guessing, I would make two comments. First, that it does not explain anything. The same conditions did not lead to monotheism with the Greek people, who were surely most gifted, but to a breaking up of polytheistic religion and to the beginning of philosophical thought. In Egypt monotheism had grown—as far as we understand its growth—as an ancillary effect of imperialism; God was the reflection of a Pharaoh autocratically governing a great world Empire. With the Jews the political conditions were most unfavourable for a development away from the idea of an exclusive national God towards that of a universal ruler of the world. Whence, then, did this tiny and impotent nation derive the audacity to pass themselves off as the favourite child of the Sovereign Lord? The question of the origin of monotheism among the Jews would thus remain unanswered or else one would have to be content with the current answer that it was the expression of their particular religious genius. We know that genius is incomprehensible and unaccountable and it should therefore not be called upon as an explanation until every other solution has failed.[1]

Furthermore, there is the fact that Jewish records and history themselves show us the way by stating emphatically—and this time without contradicting themselves—that the idea of an only God was given to the people by Moses. If there is an objection to the trustworthiness of this statement, it is that the priests, in their rewriting of the Biblical text as we have it, ascribe much too much to Moses. Institutions as well as ritualistic rules undoubtedly belonging to later times are declared to be Mosaic laws, with the clear intention of enhancing their authority. This is certainly a reason for suspicion, yet hardly enough for us to use. For the deeper motive of such an exaggeration is clear as daylight. The priests, in the accounts they present, desired to establish a continuity between their own times and the Mosaic period. They attempted to deny just what we have recognized to be the most striking feature of Jewish religious history: namely, that there was a gap between the Mosaic law-giving and the later Jewish religion—a gap filled in at first by the worship of Jahve and only later slowly covered over. Their presentation denies this sequence of events with all the means in its power, although

[1] The same consideration holds good for the remarkable case of William Shakespeare of Stratford.

its historical correctness is beyond all doubt, since throughout the peculiar treatment the Biblical text has undergone there remain more than enough statements in proof of it. The priests' version had an aim similar to that of the tendency which made the new God Jahve the God of the patriarchs. If we take into consideration this motive of the Priestly Code it is hard not to believe that it was really Moses who gave his Jews the monotheistic idea. We should find it the easier to give assent to this since we are able to say whence the idea came to Moses—something which the Jewish priesthood had certainly forgotten.

Here someone might ask what we gain by deriving Jewish monotheism from the Egyptians. The problem has thus only been put back a step; we know no more about the genesis of the monotheistic idea. The answer is that it is not a question of gain, but of research. And perhaps we shall learn something by elucidating the real process.

II. *Latency Period and Tradition*

I thus believe that the idea of an *only* God, as well as the emphasis laid on ethical demands in the name of that God and the rejection of all magic ceremonial, was indeed Mosaic doctrine, which at first found no hearing but came into its own after a long space of time and finally prevailed. How is such a delayed effect to be explained and where do we meet with similar phenomena?

Our next reflection tells us that they are often

met with in very different spheres and that they probably come about in various ways which are more or less easy to understand. Let us take for an example the fate of any new scientific theory, for instance the Darwinian doctrine of evolution. At first it meets with hostile rejection and is violently debated for decades; it takes only one generation, however, before it is recognized as a great step towards truth. Darwin himself was accorded the honour of burial in Westminster Abbey. Such a case provides no enigma. The new truth had awakened affective resistances. These could be sustained by arguments that opposed the evidence in support of the unpleasant doctrine. The contest of opinions lasted a certain time. From the very beginning there were both adherents and opponents, but the number as well as the importance of the former steadily increased until at last they gained the upper hand. During the whole time of the conflict no one forgot what was the matter at issue. We are hardly surprised to find that the whole process took a considerable time; probably we do not adequately appreciate the fact that we have here to do with a manifestation of mass psychology. There is no difficulty in finding a full analogy to it in the mental life of an individual. In such a case a person would hear of something new which, on the ground of certain evidence, he is asked to accept as true; yet it contradicts many of his wishes and offends some of his highly treasured convictions. He will then hesitate, look for arguments to cast doubt on the new material, and so struggle for a while until at last he admits it himself: "This is true after all, although I find it hard to accept and it is painful to have to believe in it." All we learn from this process is that it needs time for the intellectual work of the Ego to overcome objections that are invested by strong feelings. This case, however, is not very similar to the one we are trying to elucidate.

The next example we turn to seems to have still less in common with our problem. It may happen that someone gets away, apparently unharmed, from the spot where he has suffered a shocking accident, for instance a train collision. In the course of the following weeks, however, he develops a series of grave psychical and motor symptoms, which can be ascribed only to his shock or whatever else happened at the time of the accident. He has developed a "traumatic neurosis." This appears quite incomprehensible and is therefore a novel fact. The time that elapsed between the accident and the first appearance of the symptoms is called the "incubation period," a transparent allusion to the pathology of infectious disease. As an afterthought we observe that—in spite of the fundamental difference in the two cases, the problem of the traumatic neurosis and that of Jewish monotheism—there is a correspondence in one point. It is the feature which one might term *latency*. There are the best grounds for thinking that in the history of the Jewish religion there is a long period, after the breaking away from the Moses religion, during which no trace is to be found of the monotheistic idea, the condemnation of ceremonial, and the emphasis on the ethical side. Thus we are prepared for the possibility that the solution of our problem is to be sought in a special psychological situation.

I have more than once traced the events in Qadeš when the two components of the later Jewish people combined in the acceptance of a new religion. With those who had been in Egypt the memory of the Exodus and of the figure of Moses was still so strong and vivid that it insisted on being incorporated into any account of their early history. There might have been among them grandsons of persons who themselves had known Moses, and some of them still felt themselves to be Egyptians and bore Egyptian names. They had good reasons, however, for "repressing" the memory of the fate that had befallen their leader and lawgiver. For the other component of the tribe the leading motive was to glorify the new God and deny his foreignness. Both parties were equally concerned to deny that there had been an earlier religion and especially what it contained. This is how the first compromise came about, which probably was soon codified in writing; the people from Egypt had brought with them the art of writing and the fondness for writing history. A long time was to elapse, however, before historians came to develop an ideal of objective truth. At first they shaped their accounts according to their needs and tendencies of the moment, with an easy conscience, as if they had not yet understood what falsification signified. In consequence, a difference began to develop between the written version and the oral report—that is, the tradition—of the same subject-matter. What has been deleted or altered in the written version might quite well have been preserved uninjured in the tradition. Tradition was the complement and at the same time the contradiction of the written history. It was less subject to distorting influences—perhaps in part entirely free from them—and therefore might be more truthful than the account set down in writing. Its trustworthiness, however, was impaired by being vaguer and more fluid than the written text, being exposed to many changes and distortions as it was passed on from one generation to the next by word of mouth. Such a tradition may have different outcomes. The most likely event would be for it to be vanquished by the written version, ousted by it, until it grows more and more shadowy and at last is forgotten. Another fate might be that the tradition itself ends by becoming a written version. There are other possibilities which will be mentioned later.

The phenomenon of the latency period in the history of the Jewish religion may find its explanation in this: the facts which the so-called official written history purposely tried to suppress were in reality never lost. The knowledge of them survived in traditions which were kept alive among the people. According to Ernst Sellin, there even existed a tradition concerning the end of Moses which contradicted outright the official account and came far nearer the truth. The same thing, we may suppose, happened with other beliefs that had apparently found an end at the same time as Moses, doctrines of the Mosaic religion that had been unacceptable to the majority of Moses' contemporaries.

Here we meet with a remarkable fact. It is that these traditions, instead of growing weaker as time went on, grew more and more powerful in the course

of centuries, found their way into the later codifica-
tions of the official accounts, and at last proved themselves strong enough decisively to influence the thought
and activity of the people. What the conditions were
that made such a development possible seems, however, far from evident.

This fact is indeed strange, so much so that we
feel justified in examining it afresh. Within it our
problem lies. The Jewish people had abandoned the
Aton religion which Moses had given them and had
turned to the worship of another god who differed
little from the Baalim of the neighbouring tribes. All
the efforts of later distorting influences failed to hide
this humiliating fact. Yet the religion of Moses did
not disappear without leaving any trace; a kind of
memory of it had survived, a tradition perhaps obscured and distorted. It was this tradition of a great
past that continued to work in the background, until
it slowly gained more and more power over the mind
of the people and at last succeeded in transforming
the God Jahve into the Mosaic God and in waking to
a new life the religion which Moses had instituted
centuries before and which had later been forsaken.
That a dormant tradition should exert such a powerful influence on the spiritual life of a people is not
a familiar conception. There we find ourselves in a
domain of mass psychology where we do not feel at
home. We must look around for analogies, for facts
of a similar nature even if in other fields. We shall
find them I am sure.

When the time was ripening for a return of
the religion of Moses, the Greek people possessed an

exceptionally rich treasure of legends and myths of heroes. It is believed that the ninth or eighth century B.C. saw the creation of the Homeric epics, which derived their material from this complex of myths. With our psychological knowledge of today we could long before Schliemann and Evans have put the question: Whence did the Greeks obtain all this material of myths and legends which Homer and the great Attic dramatists transformed into immortal works of art? The answer would have had to be: This people probably passed in its early history through a period of outward splendour and highly developed culture which ended in catastrophe—as, indeed, history tells—and of which a faint tradition lived on in these legends. Archæological research of our day has confirmed this suggestion, which if made earlier would surely have been considered too bold. It has discovered the evidence of the grandiose Minoan-Mycenæan culture, which had probably already come to an end on the Greek mainland by 1250 B.C. The Greek historians of a later period hardly ever refer to it. There is the remark that there was a time when the Cretans ruled the sea, a mention of the name of King Minos and his palace, and of the labyrinth; but that is all. Nothing remained of that great time but the traditions seized upon by the great writers.

Other peoples also possess such folk-epics—for example, the Indians, Finns, and Germans. It is for the literary historian to investigate whether the same conditions as with the Greeks applied there as well. I think that such an investigation would yield a positive result. The conditions we have specified for the origin of folk-epics are as follows: there exists a period of early history that immediately afterwards is regarded as eventful, significant, grandiose, and perhaps always heroic; yet it happened so long ago and belonged to time so remote that later generations receive intelligence of it only as an obscure and incomplete tradition. Surprise has been expressed that the epic as a literary form should have disappeared in later times. The explanation may be that the conditions for the production of epics no longer exist. The old material has been used up and, so far as later events are concerned, history has taken the place of tradition. The bravest heroic deeds of our days are no longer able to inspire an epic; Alexander the Great himself had grounds for his complaint that he would have no Homer to celebrate his life.

Remote times have a great attraction—sometimes mysteriously so—for the imagination. As often as mankind is dissatisfied with its present—and that happens often enough—it harks back to the past and hopes at last to win belief in the never forgotten dream of a Golden Age.[1] Probably man still stands under the magic spell of his childhood, which a not unbiased memory presents to him as a time of unalloyed bliss. Incomplete and dim memories of the past, which we call tradition, are a great incentive to the artist, for he is free to fill in the gaps in the memories according to the behests of his imagination

[1] Such a situation forms the basis of Macaulay's *Lays of Ancient Rome*. He assumes the part of a minstrel who, sadly disappointed with the violent contests of the political parties of his time, contrasts them with the unity and patriotism of their forebears.

and to form after his own purpose the image of the time he has undertaken to reproduce. One might almost say that the more shadowy tradition has become, the more meet is it for the poet's use. The value tradition has for poetry, therefore, need not surprise us, and the analogy we have found of the dependence of epic poetry on precise conditions will make us more inclined to accept the strange suggestion that with the Jews it was the tradition of Moses that turned the Jahve-worship in the direction of the old Mosaic religion. The two cases, however, are very different in other respects. In the one the result is poetry, in the other a religion, and we have assumed that the latter —under the stimulus of a tradition—was reproduced with a faithfulness for which, of course, the epic cannot provide a parallel. Enough remains, therefore, of our problem to encourage a search for better analogies.

III. *The Analogy*

The only really satisfactory analogy to the remarkable process which we have recognized in the history of Jewish religion is to be found in a domain apparently remote from our problem. It is very complete, however, approximating to identity. Here again we find the phenomenon of latency, the appearance of inexplicable manifestations which call for an explanation, and the strict condition of an early, and subsequently forgotten, experience. Here too we find the characteristic of compulsiveness, which—overpowering logical thinking—strongly engages the psychical life;

it is a trait which was not concerned in the genesis of the epic.

This analogy is met with in psychopathology, in the genesis of human neurosis; that is to say, in a discipline belonging to individual psychology, whereas religious phenomena must of course be regarded as a part of mass psychology. We shall see that this analogy is not so startling as it appears at first sight; indeed, it is rather in the nature of an axiom.

The impressions we experienced at an early age and forgot later, to which I have ascribed such great importance for the ætiology of the neuroses, are called traumata. It may remain an open question whether the ætiology of the neuroses should in general be regarded as a traumatic one. The obvious objection is that a trauma is not always evident in the early history of the neurotic individual. Often we must be content to say that there is nothing else but an unusual reaction to experiences and demands that apply to all individuals; many people deal with them in another way which we may term normal. Where we can find no other explanation than a hereditary and constitutional disposition, we are naturally tempted to say that the neurosis was not suddenly acquired, but slowly developed.

In this connection, however, two points stand out. The first is that the genesis of the neurosis always goes back to very early impressions in childhood.[1] The second is this: it is correct to say that there are

[1] That is why it is nonsensical to maintain that psychoanalysis is practised if these early periods of life are excluded from one's investigation; yet this claim has been made in many quarters.

cases which we single out as "traumatic" ones because the effects unmistakably go back to one or more strong impressions of this early period. They failed to be disposed of normally, so that one feels inclined to say that if this or that had not happened, there would have been no neurosis. It would be sufficient for our purposes even if we had to limit the analogy in question to these traumatic cases. Yet the gap between the two groups does not seem unbridgeable. It is quite possible to combine both ætiological conditions in one conception; all depends on what is defined as traumatic. If we may assume that an experience acquires its traumatic character only in consequence of a quantitative element—that is to say, that if the experience evokes unusual pathological reactions, the fault lies in its having made too many demands on the personality—then we can formulate the conclusion that with one constitution something produces a trauma whereas with another it does not. We then have the conception of a sliding scale, a so-called complemental series, where two factors converge to complete the ætiology; a minus in one factor is compensated by a plus in the other. Generally the two factors work together and only at either end of the series can we speak of a simple motivation. In consequence of this reasoning we can leave out of account the difference between traumatic and nontraumatic ætiology as being unimportant for our analogy.

Despite some risk of repetition, it may be useful to group together the facts relating to the important analogy in question. They are as follows: Our researches have shown that what we call the phenomena or symptoms of a neurosis are the consequences of certain experiences and impressions which, for this very reason, we recognize to be ætiological traumata. We wish to ascertain, even if only in a rough schematic way, the characteristics common to these experiences and to neurotic symptoms.

Let us first consider the former. All these traumata belong to early childhood, the period up to about five years. Impressions during the time when the child begins to speak are found to be especially interesting. The period between two and four years is the most important. How soon after birth this sensitiveness to traumata begins we are not able to state with any degree of certainty.

The experiences in question are as a rule entirely forgotten and remain inaccessible to memory. They belong to the period of infantile amnesia which is often interrupted by isolated fragmentary memories, the so-called "screen-memories."

They concern impressions of a sexual and aggressive nature and also early injuries to the self (injuries to narcissism). It should be added that children at that early age do not yet distinguish between sexual and purely aggressive actions so clearly as they do later on (the "sadistic" misunderstanding of the sexual act belongs to this context). It is of course very striking that the sexual factor should predominate, and theory must take this into account.

These three points—early happenings within the first five years of life, the forgetting, and the characteristic of sexuality and aggressiveness—belong close together. The traumata are either bodily experiences or perceptions, especially those heard or seen; that is to say, they are either experiences or impressions. What connects the three points is established theoretically, by analytic work; this alone can yield a knowledge of the forgotten experiences, or—to put it more concretely, though more incorrectly—is able to bring those forgotten experiences back to memory. The theory says that, contrary to popular opinion, human sexual life—or what later corresponds to it— shows an early blossoming which comes to an end at about the age of five. Then follows the so-called latency period—lasting up to puberty—during which there is no further sexual development; on the contrary, much that had been achieved undergoes a retrogression. The theory is confirmed by anatomical study of the growth of the internal genitalia; it suggests that man is derived from a species of animal that was sexually mature at five years, and arouses the suspicion that the postponement, and the beginning twice over, of sexual life has much to do with the transition to humanity. Man seems to be the only animal with a latency period and delayed sexuality. Investigations of primates, which so far as I know have not been made, would furnish an invaluable test for this theory. It must be significant psychologically that the period of infantile amnesia coincides with this early blossoming of sexuality. Perhaps this state of affairs is a necessary condition for the existence of neurosis, which seems to be a human privilege, and which in this light appears to be a survival from primeval times—like certain parts of our body.

What features are common to all neurotic symptoms? Here we may note two important points. The effects of the trauma are twofold, positive and negative. The former are endeavours to revive the trauma, to remember the forgotten experience, or, better still, to make it real—to live through once more a repetition of it; if it was an early affective relationship it is revived in an analogous connection with another person. These endeavours are summed up in the terms "fixation to the trauma" and "repetition-compulsion." The effects can be incorporated into the so-called normal Ego and in the form of constant tendencies lend to it immutable character traits, although—or rather because—their real cause, their historical origin, has been forgotten. Thus a man who has spent his childhood in an excessive and since forgotten "mother-fixation" may all his life seek for a woman on whom he can be dependent, who will feed and keep him. A girl who was seduced in early childhood may orient her later sexual life towards provoking such assaults over and over again. It will thus be seen that to understand the problems of neurosis enables us to penetrate into the secrets of character-formation in general.

The negative reactions pursue the opposite aim; here nothing is to be remembered or repeated of the forgotten traumata. They may be grouped together as defensive reactions. They express themselves in avoiding issues, a tendency which may culminate in an inhibition or phobia. These negative reactions also contribute considerably to the formation of character. Actually they represent fixations on the trauma no less than do the positive reactions, but they follow the opposite tendency. The symptoms of the neurosis proper constitute a compromise, to which both the positive and negative effects of the trauma contribute; sometimes one component, sometimes the other, predominates. These opposite reactions create conflicts which the subject cannot as a rule resolve.

The second point is this: All these phenomena, the symptoms as well as the restrictions of personality and the lasting changes in character, display the characteristic of compulsiveness; that is to say, they possess great psychical intensity, they show a far-reaching independence of psychical processes that are adapted to the demands of the real world and obey the laws of logical thinking. They are not influenced by outer reality, or not normally so; they take no notice of real things, or the mental equivalents of these, so that they can easily come into active opposition to either. They are as a state within the state, an inaccessible party, useless for the common weal; yet they can succeed in overcoming the other the so-called normal, component and in forcing it into their service. If this happens, then the sovereignty of an inner psychical reality has been established over the reality of the outer world; the way to insanity is open. Even if it does not come to this, the practical importance of the conflict is immeasurable. The inhibitions, or even inability to deal with life, of people dominated by neurosis are a very important factor in human society. The neurosis may be regarded as a direct expression of a "fixation" to an early period of their past.

And how about latency, a question especially interesting in regard to our analogy? A trauma in childhood can be immediately followed by a neurosis during childhood; this constitutes an effort of defence accompanied by the formation of symptoms. The neurosis may last a long time and cause striking disturbances, or it may remain latent and be overlooked. As a rule, defence obtains the upper hand in such a neurosis; in any event changes of the personality remain like scars. A childhood neurosis seldom continues without an interval into the neurosis of the adult. Much more often it is succeeded by a time of undisturbed development, a process made possible or facilitated by the physiological latency. Only later does the change appear with which the neurosis becomes definitely manifest as a delayed effect of the trauma. This happens either at puberty or somewhat later. In the first case it comes about because the instincts strengthened by physical maturity can again take up the battle in which at first they were defeated. In the second case the neurosis becomes manifest later because the reactions and changes of the personality brought about by the defence mechanisms prove to be an obstacle for the solving of new problems of life, so that grave conflicts arise between the demands of the outer world and those of the Ego, which strives to preserve the organization it had painfully developed in its defensive struggle. The phenomenon of a latency in the neurosis between the first reactions to the trauma and the later appearance of the illness must be recognized as typical. The illness may also be regarded as an attempt at cure, an endeavour to reconcile the divided Ego—divided by the trauma—with the rest and to unite it into a strong whole that will be fit to cope with the outer world. Yet such an effort is rarely successful unless analytic help is sought, and even then not always. Often it ends in entirely destroying and breaking up the Ego or in the Ego being overpowered by the portion that was early split off, and has since been dominated, by the trauma.

To convince the reader of the truth of these statements the exhaustive communication of several neurotic life-histories would be necessary. The difficulty of the subject, however, would lead to great discursiveness and entirely destroy the character of this essay. It would become a treatise on the neuroses and even then would enforce conviction only on that minority of people who have devoted their life's work to the study and practice of psychoanalysis. Since I am speaking here to a larger audience, I can only ask the reader to lend a tentative credence to the abbreviated exposition which he has just read; I, on my part, agree that he need accept the deductions which I propose to lay before him only if the theories on which they are based turn out to be correct.

Nevertheless I can try to relate one case which will show clearly many of the peculiarities of neurosis that I have mentioned above. One case cannot, of course, display everything; so I shall not be disappointed if its content seems far away from the analogy we are seeking.

A little boy who, as so often happens in the families of the lower middle class, shared his parents' bedroom had ample, and even regular, opportunity for observing sexual intercourse at an age before he was able to talk. He saw much and heard still more.

In his later neurosis, which broke out immediately after the time of his first seminal emission, disturbed sleep was the earliest and most trying symptom. He became extraordinarily sensitive to nocturnal noises and, if once awakened, could not get to sleep again. This disturbance was a true compromise symptom: on the one hand the expression of his defence against his nocturnal observations, on the other hand the endeavour to re-establish the wakefulness which had enabled him to listen to those experiences.

Stirred early to aggressive virility by these observations, the boy began to excite his penis by touch and to make sexual advances towards his mother, putting himself thus in his father's place through identification with him. This went on until at last his mother forbade him to touch his penis and threatened to tell his father, who would take the offending organ away. This threat of castration had a very strong traumatic effect on the boy. He relinquished his sexual activity, and his character underwent a change. Instead of identifying himself with his father he began to be afraid of him, adopted a passive attitude towards him, and by means of occasional disobedience provoked his father to punish him physically. This corporal punishment had sexual significance for him and in that way he could identify himself with the ill-treated mother. He began to cling more and more closely to his mother as if he could not bear to be without her love, even for a moment, since this constituted a protection against the danger of castration from his father. The latency period was spent in this

modification of the Œdipus complex; it remained free
from obvious disturbances. He became a model child
and was successful in school.

So far we have pursued the immediate effect
of the trauma and confirmed the existence of a latency period.

The appearance of puberty brought with it the
manifest neurosis and disclosed its second main symptom, sexual impotency. He had lost all sensitiveness
in his penis, never tried to touch it, and never dared
to approach a woman sexually. His sexual activities
remained restricted to psychical onanism with sadistic-
masochistic phantasies in which it was easy to recognize the consequence of those early observations of
parental coitus. The thrust of increased virility that
puberty brought with it turned to ferocious hatred of
his father and opposition to him. This extreme negative relation to his father, which went as far as injur-
ing his own interests, was the reason for his failure in
life and his conflicts with the outer world. He could
not allow himself to be successful in his profession
because his father had forced him to adopt it. He
made no friends and was always on bad terms with
his superiors.

Burdened with these symptoms and incapacities,
he found at last a wife after his father's death. Then
the core of his character appeared, traits which made
him very difficult to live with. He developed an absolutely egotistical, despotic, and brutal personality;
it was obviously necessary to him to bully and oppress
other people. He was the exact copy of his father,
after the image of him he had formed in his memory;

that is to say, he revived the father-identification which as a child he had adopted for sexual motives. In this part of the neurosis we recognize the return of the repressed, which—with the immediate effects of the trauma and the phenomenon of latency—I have described as among the essential symptoms of a neurosis.

IV. *Application*

Early trauma—defence—latency—outbreak of the neurosis—partial return of the repressed material: this was the formula we drew up for the development of a neurosis. Now I will invite the reader to take a step forward and assume that in the history of the human species something happened similar to the events in the life of the individual. That is to say, mankind as a whole also passed through conflicts of a sexual-aggressive nature which left permanent traces, but which were for the most part warded off and forgotten, later after a long period of latency, they came to life again and created phenomena similar in structure and tendency to neurotic symptoms.

I have, I believe, divined these processes and wish to show that their consequences, which bear a strong resemblance to neurotic symptoms, are the phenomena of religion. Since it can no longer be doubted after the discovery of evolution that mankind had a prehistory, and since this history is unknown (that is to say, forgotten), such a conclusion has almost the significance of an axiom. If we should learn that the effective and forgotten traumata relate, here as well as there, to life in the human family, we should greet this information as a highly welcome and unforeseen gift which could not have been anticipated from the foregoing discussion.

I have already upheld this thesis, a quarter of a century ago, in my book *Totem and Taboo* (1912), and need only repeat what I said there. The argument started from some remarks by Charles Darwin and embraced a suggestion of Atkinson's. It says that in primeval times men lived in small hordes, each under the domination of a strong male. When this was is not known; no point of contact with geological data has been established. It is likely that mankind was not very far advanced in the art of speech. An essential part of the argument is that all primeval men, including, therefore, all our ancestors, underwent the fate I shall now describe.

The story is told in a very condensed way, as if what in reality took centuries to achieve, and during that long time was repeated innumerably, had happened only once. The strong male was the master and father of the whole horde, unlimited in his power, which he used brutally. All females were his property, the wives and daughters in his own horde as well as perhaps also those stolen from other hordes. The fate of the sons was a hard one; if they excited the father's jealousy they were killed or castrated or driven out. They were forced to live in small communities and to provide themselves with wives by stealing them from others. Then one or the other son might succeed in attaining a situation similar to that of the father in the original horde. One favoured position came about in a natural way: it was that of the youngest son, who, protected by his mother's love, could profit by his father's advancing years and replace him after his death. An echo of the expulsion of the eldest son, as well as of the favoured position of the youngest, seems to linger in many myths and fairy-tales.

The next decisive step towards changing this first kind of "social" organization lies in the following suggestion: the brothers who had been driven out and lived together in a community clubbed together, overcame the father, and—according to the custom of those times—all partook of his body. This cannibalism need not shock us, it survived into far later times. The essential point is, however, that we attribute to those primeval people the same feelings and emotions that we have elucidated in the primitives of our own times, our children, by psychoanlytic research. That is to say, they not merely hated and feared their father, but also honoured him as an example to follow; in fact, each son wanted to place himself in his father's position. The cannibalistic act thus becomes comprehensible as an attempt to assure one's identification with the father by incorporating a part of him.

It is a reasonable surmise that after the killing of the father a time followed when the brothers quarrelled among themselves for the succession, which each of them wanted to obtain for himself alone. They came to see that these fights were as dangerous as they were futile. This hard-won understanding—as well as the memory of the deed of liberation they had achieved together and the attachment that had grown up among them during the time of their exile—led at last to a union among them, a sort of social contract. Thus there came into being the first form of a social organization accompanied by a renunciation of instinctual gratification; recognition of mutual obligations; institutions declared sacred, which could not be broken—in short, the beginnings of morality and law. Each renounced the ideal of gaining for himself the position of father, of possessing his mother or sister. With this the taboo of incest and the law of exogamy came into being. A good part of the power which had become vacant through the father's death passed to the women; the time of the matriarchate followed. The memory of the father lived on during this time of the "brother horde." A strong animal, which perhaps at first was also dreaded, was found as a substitute. Such a choice may seem very strange to us, but the gulf which man created later between himself and the animals did not exist for primitive man. Nor does it with our children, whose animal phobias we have been able to explain as dread of the father. The relationship to the totem animal retained the original ambivalency of feeling towards the father. The totem was, on the one hand, the corporeal ancestor and protecting spirit of the clan; he was to be revered and protected. On the other hand, a festival was instituted on which day the same fate was meted out to him as the primeval father had encountered. He was killed and eaten by all the brothers together (the totem feast, according to Robertson Smith). This great day was in reality a feast of triumph to celebrate the victory of the united sons over the father.

Where, in this connection, does religion come in? Totemism, with its worship of a father substitute, the ambivalency towards the father which is evidenced by the totem feast, the institution of remembrance festivals and of laws the breaking of which is punished by death—this totemism, I conclude, may be regarded as the earliest appearance of religion in the history of mankind, and it illustrates the close connection existing from the very beginning of time between social institutions and moral obligations. The further development of religion can be treated here only in a very summary fashion. Without a doubt it proceeded parallel to the cultural development of mankind and the changes in the structure of human social institutions.

The next step forward from totemism is the humanizing of the worshipped being. Human gods, whose origin in the totem is not veiled, take the place previously filled by animals. Either the god is still represented as an animal or at least he bears the countenance of an animal; the totem may become the inseparable companion of the god, or, again, the myth makes the god vanquish just that animal which was nothing but his predecessor. At one period—it is hard to say when—great mother deities appeared, probably before the male gods, and they were worshipped beside the latter for a long time to come. During that time a great social revolution had taken place. Matriarchy was followed by a restitution of the patriarchal order. The new fathers, it is true, never succeeded to the omnipotence of the primeval father. There were too many of them and they lived in larger communities than the original horde had been; they had to get on with one another and were restricted by social institutions. Probably the mother deities were developed when the matriarchy was being limited, in order to compensate the dethroned mothers. The male gods appear at first as sons by the side of the great mothers; only later do they clearly assume the features of the father. These male gods of polytheism mirror the conditions of patriarchal times. They are numerous, they have to share their authority, and occasionally they obey a higher god. The next step, however, leads us to the topic that interests us here: the return of the one and only father deity whose power is unlimited.

I must admit that this historical survey leaves many a gap and in many points needs further confirmation. Yet whoever declares this reconstruction of primeval history to be fantastic greatly under-estimates the richness and the force of the evidence that has gone to make it up. Large portions of the past, which are here woven into a whole, are historically proved or even show their traces to this day, such as matriarchal right, totemism, and male communities. Others have survived in remarkable replicas. Thus more than one author has been struck by the close resemblance between the rite of Christian Communion—where the believer symbolically incorporates the blood and flesh of his God—and the totem feast, whose inner meaning it reproduces. Numerous survivals of our forgotten early history are preserved in the legends and fairytales of the peoples, and analytic study of the mental life of the child has yielded an unexpectedly rich return by filling up gaps in our knowledge of primeval times. As a contribution towards an understanding of the highly important relation between father and son I need only quote the animal phobias, the fear of being eaten by the father (which seems so strange to the grown mind), and the enormous intensity of the castration complex. There is nothing in our reconstruction that is invented, nothing that is not based on good grounds.

Let us suppose that the presentation here given of primeval history is on the whole credible. Then two elements can be recognized in religious rites and doctrines: on the one hand, fixations on the old family-history and survivals of this; on the other hand, reproductions of the past and a return long after of what had been forgotten. It is the latter element that has until now been overlooked and therefore not understood. It will therefore be illustrated here by at least one impressive example.

It is specially worthy of note that every memory returning from the forgotten past does so with great force, produces an incomparably strong influence on the mass of mankind, and puts forward an irresistible claim to be believed, against which all logical objections remain powerless—very much like the *credo quia absurdum*. This strange characteristic can only be understood by comparison with the delusions in a psychotic case. It has long been recognized that delusions contain a piece of forgotten truth, which had at its return to put up with being distorted and misunderstood, and that the compulsive conviction appertaining to the delusion emanates from this core of truth and spreads to the errors that enshroud it. Such a kernel of truth—which we might call *historical* truth—must also be conceded to the doctrines of the various religions. They are, it is true, imbued with the character of psychotic symptoms, but as mass phenomena they have escaped the curse of isolation.

No other part of religious history has become so abundantly clear as the establishment of monotheism among the Jewish people and its continuation into Christianity—if we omit the development from the animal totem to the human god with his regular (animal) companion, a development which can be traced without a gap and readily understood. (Each of the four Christian Evangelists, by the way, still has his favourite animal.) If we admit for the moment that the rule of Pharaoh's Empire was the external reason for the appearance of the monotheistic idea, we see that this idea—uprooted from its soil and transplanted to another people—after a long latency period takes hold of this people, is treasured by them as their most precious possession, and for its part keeps this people alive by bestowing on them the pride of being the chosen people. It is the religion of the primeval father, and the hope of reward, distinction, and finally world sovereignty is bound up with it. The last-named wish-phantasy—relinquished long ago by the Jewish people—still survives among their enemies in their belief in the conspiracy of the "Elders of Zion." We shall consider in a later chapter how the special peculiarities of a monotheistic religion borrowed from Egypt must have worked on the Jewish people, how it formed their character for good through the disdaining of magic and mysticism and encouraging them to progress in spirituality and sublimations. The people, happy in their conviction of possessing truth, overcome by the consciousness of being the chosen, came to value highly all intellectual and ethical achievements. I shall also show how their sad fate, and the disappointments reality had in store for them, were able to strengthen all these tendencies. At present, however, we shall follow their historical development in another direction.

The restoration to the primeval father of his historical rights marked a great progress, but this could not be the end. The other parts of the prehistoric tragedy also clamoured for recognition. How this process was set in motion it is not easy to say. It seems that a growing feeling of guiltiness had seized the Jewish people—and perhaps the whole of civilization of that time—as a precursor of the return of the repressed material. This went on until a member of the Jewish people, in the guise of a political-religious agitator, founded a doctrine which—together with another one, the Christian religion—separated from the Jewish one. Paul, a Roman Jew from Tarsus, seized upon this feeling of guilt and correctly traced it back to its primeval source. This he called original sin; it was a crime against God that could be expiated only through death. Death had come into the world through original sin. In reality this crime, deserving of death, had been the murder of the Father who later was deified. The murderous deed itself, however, was not remembered; in its place stood the phantasy of expiation, and that is why this phantasy could be welcomed in the form of a gospel of salvation (evangel). A Son of God, innocent himself, had sacrificed himself, and had thereby taken over the guilt of the world. It had to be a Son, for the sin had been murder of the Father. Probably traditions from Oriental and Greek mysteries had exerted their influence on the shaping of this phantasy of salvation. The essence of it seems to be Paul's own contribution. He was a man with a gift for religion, in the truest sense of the phrase. Dark traces of the past lay in his soul, ready to break through into the regions of consciousness.

That the Redeemer sacrificed himself as an innocent man was an obviously tendentious distortion, difficult to reconcile with logical thinking. How could a man who was innocent assume the guilt of the murderer by allowing himself to be killed? In historical reality there was no such contradiction. The "redeemer" could be no one else but he who was most guilty, the leader of the brother horde who had overpowered the Father. Whether there had been such a chief rebel and leader must, in my opinion, remain uncertain. It is quite possible, but we must also consider that each member of the brother horde certainly had the wish to do the deed by himself and thus to create for himself a unique position as a substitute for the identification with the father which he had to give up when he was submerged in the community. If there was no such leader, then Christ was the heir of an unfulfilled wish-phantasy; if there was such

a leader, then Christ was his successor and his rein-
carnation. It is unimportant, however, whether we
have here a phantasy or the return of a forgotten
reality; in any case, here lies the origin of the conception of the hero—him who rebels against the father
and kills him in some guise or other.[1] Here we also
find the real source of the "tragic guilt" of the hero
in drama—a guilt hard to demonstrate otherwise. We
can hardly doubt that in Greek tragedy the hero and
the chorus represent this same rebel hero and the
brother horde, and it cannot be without significance
that in the Middle Ages the theatre began afresh with
the story of the Passion.

I have already mentioned that the Christian
ceremony of Holy Communion, in which the believer
incorporates the flesh and blood of the Redeemer, re-
peats the content of the old totem feast; it does so, it
is true, only in its tender and adoring sense, not in
its aggressive sense. The ambivalency dominating the
father-son relationship shows clearly, however, in the
final result of the religious innovation. Meant to pro-
pitiate the Father Deity, it ends by his being dethroned and set aside. The Mosaic religion had been
a Father religion; Christianity became a Son religion.
The old God, the Father, took second place; Christ, the
Son, stood in his stead, just as in those dark times
every son had longed to do. Paul, by developing the
Jewish religion further, became its destroyer. His suc-

---

[1] Ernest Jones calls my attention to the probability that
the god Mithra, who slays the Bull, represented this leader, the
one who simply gloried in his deed. It is well known how long
the worship of Mithra disputed the final victory with Christianity.

cess was certainly mainly due to the fact that through the idea of salvation he laid the ghost of the feeling of guilt. It was also due to his giving up the idea of the chosen people and its visible sign—circumcision. That is how the new religion could become all-embracing, universal. Although this step might have been determined by Paul's revengefulness on account of the opposition which his innovation found among the Jews, nevertheless one characteristic of the old Aton religion (universality) was reinstated; a restriction had been abolished which it had acquired while passing on to a new carrier, the Jewish people.

In certain respects the new religion was a cultural regression as compared with the older Jewish religion; this happens regularly when a new mass of people of a lower cultural level effects an invasion or is admitted into an older culture. The Christian religion did not keep to the lofty heights of spirituality to which the Jewish religion had soared. The former was no longer strictly monotheistic; it took over from the surrounding peoples numerous symbolical rites, re-established the great mother goddess, and found room for many deities of polytheism in an easily recognizable disguise, though in subordinate positions. Above all it was not inaccessible, as the Aton religion and the subsequent Mosaic religion had been, to the penetration of superstitions, magical and mystical elements which proved a great hindrance to the spiritual development of two following millennia.

The triumph of Christianity was a renewed victory of the Ammon priests over the God of Ikhnaton after an interval of a millennium and a half and over a larger region. And yet Christianity marked a progress in the history of religion: that is to say, in regard to the return of the repressed. From now on, the Jewish religion was, so to speak, a fossil.

It would be worth while to understand why the monotheistic idea should make such a deep impression on just the Jewish people, and why they adhered to it so tenaciously. I believe this question can be answered. The great deed and misdeed of primeval times, the murder of the father, was brought home to the Jews, for fate decreed that they should repeat it on the person of Moses, an eminent father substitute. It was a case of acting instead of remembering, something which often happens during analytic work with neurotics. They responded to the doctrine of Moses—which should have been a stimulus to their memory—by denying their act, did not progress beyond the recognition of the great father, and barred the passage to the point where later on Paul started his continuation of primeval history. It can scarcely be chance that the violent death of another great man should become the starting-point for the creation of a new religion by Paul. This was a man whom a small number of adherents in Judea believed to be the Son of God and the promised Messiah, and who later on took over some of the childhood history that had been attached to Moses. In reality, however, we have hardly more definite knowledge of him than we have of Moses. We do not know if he was really the great man whom the Gospels depict or whether it was not rather the fact and the circumstances of his death that were the decisive factor in his achieving importance. Paul, who became his apostle, did not himself know him.

The murder of Moses by his people—which Sellin recognized in the traces of tradition and which, strangely enough, the young Goethe[1] had assumed without any evidence—has thus become an indispensable part of our reasoning, an important link between the forgotten deed of primeval times and its subsequent reappearance in the form of monotheistic religions.[2] It is an attractive suggestion that the guilt attached to the murder of Moses may have been the stimulus for the wish-phantasy of the Messiah, who was to return and give to his people salvation and the promised sovereignty over the world. If Moses was this first Messiah, Christ became his substitute and successor. Then Paul could with a certain right say to the peoples: "See, the Messiah has truly come. He was indeed murdered before your eyes." Then also there is some historical truth in the rebirth of Christ, for he was the resurrected Moses and the returned primeval father of the primitive horde as well—only transfigured, and as a Son in the place of his Father.

The poor Jewish people, who with its usual stiff-necked obduracy continued to deny the murder of their "father," has dearly expiated this in the course of centuries. Over and over again they heard the reproach: "You killed our God." And this reproach

[1] *Israel in der Wüste,* Vol. VII of the Weimar edition, p. 170.

[2] Compare in this connection the well-known exposition in Frazer's *The Golden Bough,* Part III, "The Dying God" (1911).

is true, if rightly interpreted. It says, in reference to the history of religion: "You won't *admit* that you murdered God" (the archetype of God, the primeval Father, and his reincarnations). Something should be added—namely: "It is true, we did the same thing, but we *admitted* it, and since then we have been purified." Not all accusations with which anti-Semitism pursues the descendants of the Jewish people are based on such good foundations. There must, of course, be more than one reason for a phenomenon of such intensity and lasting strength as the popular hatred of Jews. A whole series of reasons can be divined; some of them, which need no interpretation, arise from obvious considerations; others lie deeper and spring from secret sources, which one would regard as the specific motives. In the first group the most fallacious is the reproach of their being foreigners, since in many places nowadays under the sway of anti-Semitism the Jews were the oldest constituents of the population or arrived even before the present inhabitants. This is so, for example, in the town of Cologne, where Jews came with the Romans, before it was colonized by Germanic tribes. Other grounds for anti-Semitism are stronger, as, for example, the circumstance that Jews mostly live as a minority among other peoples, since the feeling of solidarity of the masses, in order to be complete, has need of an animosity against an outside minority, and the numerical weakness of the minority invites suppression. Two other peculiarities that the Jews possess, however, are quite unpardonable. The first is that in many respects they are different from their "hosts."

Not fundamentally so, since they are not a foreign Asiatic race, as their enemies maintain, but mostly consist of the remnants of Mediterranean peoples and inherit their culture. Yet they are different—although sometimes it is hard to define in what respects—especially from the Nordic peoples, and racial intolerance finds stronger expression, strange to say, in regard to small differences than to fundamental ones. The second peculiarity has an even more pronounced effect. It is that they defy oppression, that even the most cruel persecutions have not succeeded in exterminating them. On the contrary, they show a capacity for holding their own in practical life and, where they are admitted, they make valuable contributions to the surrounding civilization.

The deeper motives of anti-Semitism have their roots in times long past; they come from the unconscious, and I am quite prepared to hear that what I am going to say will at first appear incredible. I venture to assert that the jealousy which the Jews evoked in other peoples by maintaining that they were the first-born, favourite child of God the Father has not yet been overcome by those others, just as if the latter had given credence to the assumption. Furthermore, among the customs through which the Jews marked off their aloof position, that of circumcision made a disagreeable, uncanny impression on others. The explanation probably is that it reminds them of the dreaded castration idea and of things in their primeval past which they would fain forget. Then there is lastly the most recent motive of the series. We must not forget that all the peoples who now excel in the practice of anti-Semitism became Christians only in relatively recent times, sometimes forced to it by bloody compulsion. One might say they all are "badly christened"; under the thin veneer of Christianity they have remained what their ancestors were, barbarically polytheistic. They have not yet overcome their grudge against the new religion which was forced on them, and they have projected it on to the source from which Christianity came to them. The facts that the Gospels tell a story which is enacted among Jews, and in truth treats only of Jews, has facilitated such a projection. The hatred for Judaism is at bottom hatred for Christianity, and it is not surprising that in the German National Socialist revolution this close connection of the two monotheistic religions finds such clear expression in the hostile treatment of both.

v. *Difficulties*

Perhaps the preceding chapter has succeeded in establishing the analogy between neurotic processes and religious events and thereby in pointing to the unexpected origin of the latter. In this translation from individual into mass psychology two difficulties emerge, different in nature and importance, which we must now examine. The first is that we have treated here of only one case in the rich phenomenology of religions and have not thrown any light on the others I regretfully have to admit that I cannot give more than one sample, that I have not the expert knowledge necessary to complete the investigation. This limited knowledge will allow me perhaps to add that the founding of the Mohammedan religion seems to me to be an abbreviated repetition of the Jewish one, in imitation of which it made its appearance. There is reason to believe that the Prophet originally intended to accept the Jewish religion in full for himself and his people. The regaining of the one great primeval Father produced in the Arabs an extraordinary advance in self-confidence which led them to great worldly successes, but which, it is true, exhausted itself in these. Allah proved himself to be much more grateful to his chosen people than Jahve had in his time. The inner development of the new religion, however, soon came to a standstill, perhaps because it lacked the profundity which in the Jewish religion resulted from the murder of its founder. The apparently rationalistic religions of the East are in essence ancestor cults; therefore they stop short at an early stage of the reconstruction of the past. If it is correct that in the primitive peoples of our time we find as the sole content of their religion the worship of a highest Being, then we can interpret this only as a withering in the development of religion, and from here draw a parallel with the innumerable cases of rudimentary neuroses which we find in clinical psychology. Why here as well as there no further development took place, we do not understand. We must hold the individual gifts of these peoples responsible for it, the direction their activities take and their general social condition. Besides, it is a good rule in analytic work to be satisfied with explaining what exists and not to try to explain what has not happened.

The second difficulty in this translation into mass psychology is much more significant, because it presents a new problem of a cardinal nature. The question arises in what form is the active tradition in the life of the peoples still extant. There is no such question with individuals, for here the matter is settled by the existence of memory traces of the past in the unconscious. Let us go back to our historical example. The compromise in Qadeš, I said, was based on the continued existence of a powerful tradition living on in the people who had returned from Egypt. There is no problem here. I suggested that such a tradition was maintained by conscious memory of oral communications which had been passed on from forebears of only two or three generations before. The latter had been participants and eyewitnesses of the events in question. Can we believe the same, however, for the later centuries—namely, that the tradition was always based on a knowledge, communicated in a normal way, which had been transmitted from forebear to descendant? Who the persons were that stored such knowledge and passed it on from mouth to mouth we no longer know, as we did in the earlier case. According to Sellin, the tradition of the murder of Moses was always present among the priests, until at last it was set down in writing, which alone made it possible for Sellin to divine it. Yet it could not have been known to many; it was not general knowledge. And is this form of transmission enough to explain its effect? Can we credit such a knowledge on the part of a few with the power to seize the imagination of the masses so lastingly when they learn of it? It rather looks as if there were something also in the ignorant mass of the people akin to this knowledge on the part of the few, which comes forward to meet it as soon as it is uttered.

It becomes harder still to arrive at a conclusion when we turn to the analogous case in primeval times. In the course of thousands of centuries it certainly became forgotton that there was a primeval father possessing the qualities I mentioned, and what fate he met. Nor can we assume an oral tradition as we did with Moses. In what sense, therefore, can there be any question of a tradition? In what form could it have existed?

To help readers who are unwilling or unprepared to plunge into complicated psychological matters, I shall place the result of the following investigation at the very beginning. I hold that the concordance between the individual and the mass is in this point almost complete. The masses, too, retain an impression of the past in unconscious memory traces.

The case of the individual seems to be clear enough. The memory trace of early events he has retained, but he has retained it in a special psychological condition. One may say that the individual always knew of them, in the sense that we know repressed material. We have formed certain conceptions —and they can easily be proved by analysis—of how something gets forgotten and of how after a time it can come to light again. The forgotten material is not extinguished. only "repressed"; its traces are extant in the memory in their original freshness, but they are isolated by "counter-cathexes." They cannot establish contact with the other intellectual processes; they are unconscious, inaccessible to consciousness. It may happen that certain parts of the repressed material have escaped this process, have remained accessible to memory and occasionally reappear in consciousness, but even then they are isolated, a foreign body without any connection with the rest of the mind. This may happen, but it need not happen. Repression may also be complete, and this is the case I propose to examine.

This repressed material retains its impetus to penetrate into consciousness. It reaches its aim when three conditions are present: (1) When the strength of counter-cathexis is diminished by an illness which acts on the Ego itself, or through a different distribution of cathexis in the Ego, as happens regularly during sleep. (2) When those instincts attached to the repressed material become strengthened. The processes during puberty provide the best example for this. (3) Whenever recent events produce impressions or experiences which are so much like the repressed material that they have the power to awaken it. Thus the recent material gets strengthened by the latent energy of the repressed, and the repressed material produces its effect behind the recent material and with its help.

In none of the three cases does the material that had been repressed succeed in reaching consciousness unimpeded or without change. It must always undergo distortions which bear witness to the not entirely overcome resistance derived from the counter-cathexis, or else to the modifying influence of a recent experience, or to both.

As a distinguishing sign and landmark I have used the difference between a psychic process being conscious or unconscious. The repressed material is unconscious. It would be a cheering simplification if this sentence could be reversed—that is, if the difference of the qualities "conscious" and "unconscious" were identical with the difference "belonging to the Ego" or "repressed." The fact that our mental life harboured such isolated and unconscious material would be new and important enough. In reality things are more complex. It is true that all repressed material is unconscious, but not true that everything belonging to the Ego is conscious. We become aware that being conscious is an ephemeral quality which adheres to a psychical process only temporarily. This is why for our purposes we must replace "conscious" by "capable of being conscious," and we call this quality "preconscious." We then say more correctly: the Ego is essentially preconscious (virtually conscious), but parts of the Ego are unconscious

This last statement teaches us that the qualities to which we have attended so far do not suffice to show us the way in the darkness of mental life. We must introduce another distinction, one no longer qualitative, but topographical, and—which lends it a special value—genetic at the same time. Now we distinguish from our mental life—which we see to be an apparatus consisting of several hierarchies, districts, or provinces—one region, which we term the "real

Ego," from another which we call the "Id." The Id is the older; the Ego has developed out of it through the influence of the outer world as the bark develops around a tree. Our primary instincts start in the Id; all processes in the Id are unconscious. The Ego corresponds, as I have mentioned, with the realm of the preconscious; parts of it normally remain unconscious. The psychical processes in the "Id" obey quite different laws; their course and the influence they exert on one another are different from those that reign in the Ego. It is the discovery of these differences that has guided us to our new understanding and lends confirmation to it.

The repressed material must be regarded as belonging to the Id and obeys its mechanisms; it differs from it only in respect of its genesis. This differentiation takes place during the early period, while the Ego is developing out of the Id. Then the Ego takes possession of part of the Id and raises it to the preconscious level; other parts are thus not affected and remain in the Id as the "unconscious" proper. In the further development of the Ego, however, certain psychical impressions and processes in it get shut out by defensive mechanisms; they are deprived of their preconscious character, so that they are degraded again to become integral parts of the Id. This, therefore, is the "repressed material" in the Id. As regards the passage between the two mental provinces we assume, on the one hand, that unconscious processes in the Id can be raised to a preconscious level and incorporated into the Ego, and, on the other hand, that preconscious material in the Ego can travel the opposite way and be shifted back into the Id. That, later on, another district, the "Super-ego," is delimited in the Ego does not concern us in this context.

All this may seem far from simple, but if one has become familiar with the unaccustomed topographical conception of the mental apparatus, then there are no particular difficulties. I will add here that the topography of the psyche I have here developed has in general nothing to do with cerebral anatomy; there is only one point where it impinges on it. The unsatisfactoriness of this conception—which I perceive as clearly as anyone—has its roots in our complete ignorance of the dynamic nature of mental processes. We realize that what distinguishes a conscious idea from a preconscious one, and this from an unconscious one, cannot be anything but a modification, or perhaps also another distribution, of psychic energy. We speak of cathexes and hypercathexes, but beyond this we lack all knowledge and even a beginning for a useful working hypothesis. Of the phenomenon of consciousness we are at least able to say that it cleaves originally to perception. All perceptions which come about through painful, tactile, auditory, or visual stimuli are the more likely to be conscious. Thought-processes, and what may be analogous to them in the Id, are unconscious *per se* and obtain their entry into consciousness by their connection, via the function of speech, with memory traces of perceptions through touch and ear. In the animal, which lacks speech, these relationships must be simpler.

The impressions of the early traumata, from

which we started, either are not translated into the preconscious or they are soon redirected into the Id through repression. Their memory residues are then unconscious and operate from the Id. We believe we can follow their further fate distinctly as long as they deal with personal experiences. A new complication arises, however, when we become aware that there probably exists in the mental life of the individual not only what he has experienced himself, but also what he brought with him at birth, fragments of phylogenetic origin, an archaic heritage. Then the question arises: in what does this inheritance consist, what does it contain, and what evidence of it is there?

The first and most certain answer is that it consists in certain dispositions, such as all living beings possess; that is to say, in the ability and tendency to follow a certain direction of development and to react in a particular way to certain excitations, impressions, and stimuli. Since experience shows that individuals differ in this respect, our archaic inheritance includes these differences; they represent what is recognized as the constitutional element in the individual. Since all human beings go through the same experiences, at least in their earliest years, they also react to them in the same way, and this is why the doubt arose whether these reactions with all their individual differences should not be reckoned as part of that archaic heritage. This doubt must be rejected; the fact of this similarity does not enrich our knowledge of the archaic heritage.

Meanwhile analytic research has yielded several

results which give us food for thought. First of all there is the universality of speech symbolism. Symbolic substitution of one object through another—the same applies to actions—our children are conversant with, and it seems quite natural to them. We cannot trace the way in which they learned it and must admit that in many cases to learn it would be impossible. It is original knowledge, which the adult later on forgets. He employs, it is true, the same symbolism in his dreams, but he does not understand them unless the analyst interprets them for him, and even then he is loath to believe the translation. When he has used one of the common phrases of speech in which this symbolism is crystallized, he has to admit that its true meaning had quite escaped him. Symbolism even ignores the difference in languages; investigation would probably show that it is ubiquitous, the same with all peoples. Here there seems to be an assured case of archaic inheritance from the time when speech was developing, although one might attempt another explanation: one might say that these are thought-connections between ideas which were formed during the historical development of speech and which have to be repeated every time the individual passes through such a development. This then would be a case of inheriting a thought-disposition as elsewhere one inherits an instinctual disposition; so it again would contribute nothing new to our problem.

Analytic research, however, has also brought to light other things, which exceed in significance anything we have so far discussed. In studying reactions to early traumata we often find to our surprise that they do not keep strictly to what the individual himself has experienced, but deviate from this in a way that would accord much better with their being reactions to genetic events and in general can be explained only through such an influence. The behaviour of a neurotic child to his parents when under the influence of an Œdipus and castration complex is very rich in such reactions, which seem unreasonable in the individual and can only be understood phylogenetically, in relation to the experiences of earlier generations. It would be amply worth while to collect and publish the material on which my remarks are based. In fact it seems to me convincing enough to allow me to venture further and assert that the archaic heritage of mankind includes not only dispositions, but also ideational contents, memory traces of the experiences of former generations. In this way the extent as well as the significance of the archaic heritage would be enhanced in a remarkable degree.

On second thoughts I must admit that I have argued as if there were no question that there exists an inheritance of memory—traces of what our forefathers experienced, quite independently of direct communication and of the influence of education by example. When I speak of an old tradition still alive in a people, of the formation of a national character, it is such an inherited tradition, and not one carried on by word of mouth, that I have in mind. Or at least I did not distinguish between the two, and was not quite clear about what a bold step I took by neglecting this difference. This state of affairs is made more difficult, it is true, by the present attitude of biological science, which rejects the idea of acquired qualities being transmitted to descendants. I admit, in all modesty, that in spite of this I cannot picture biological development proceeding without taking this factor into account. The two cases, it is true, are not quite similar; with the former, it is a question of acquired qualities that are hard to conceive; with the latter, memory traces of external expressions, something almost concrete. Probably, however, we cannot *au fond* imagine one without the other. If we accept the continued existence of such memory traces in our archaic inheritance, then we have bridged the gap between individual and mass psychology and can treat peoples as we do the individual neurotic. Though we may admit that for the memory traces in our archaic inheritance we have so far no stronger proof than those remnants of memory evoked by analytic work, which call for a derivation from phylogenesis, yet this proof seems to me convincing enough to postulate such a state of affairs. If things are different, then we are unable to advance one step further on our way, either in psychoanalysis or in mass psychology. It is bold, but inevitable.

In making this postulate we also do something else. We diminish the over-wide gap human arrogance in former times created between man and beast. If the so-called instincts of animals—which from the very beginning allow them to behave in their new conditions of living as if they were old and long-established ones—if this instinctual life of animals permits of any explanation at all, it can only be this: that they carry over into their new existence the experience of their kind; that is to say, that they have preserved in their minds memories of what their ancestors experienced. In the human animal things should not be fundamentally different. His own archaic heritage, though different in extent and character, corresponds to the instincts of animals.

After these considerations I have no qualms in saying that men have always known—in this particular way—that once upon a time they had a primeval father and killed him.

Two further questions must here be answered. First, under what conditions does such a memory enter into the archaic inheritance; and, secondly, in what circumstances can it become active—that is to say, penetrate from its unconscious state in the Id into consciousness, though in an altered and distorted form? The answer to the first question is easy to formulate: it happens when the experience is important enough, or is repeated often enough, or in both cases. With the father-murder both conditions are fulfilled. To the second question I would remark: there may be a number of influences which need not all be known; a spontaneous course is also possible in analogy with what happens in some neuroses. The awakening, however, of the memory trace through a recent real repetition of the event is certainly of decisive importance. The murder of Moses was such a repetition and, later on, the supposed judicial murder of Christ, so that these events move into the foreground as causative agents. It seems as if the genesis of monotheism would not have been possible without these events. We are reminded of the words of the poet:

> *All that is to live in endless song*
> *Must in life-time first be drown'd.*[1]

I will conclude with a remark which furnishes a psychological argument. A tradition based only on oral communication could not produce the obsessive character which appertains to religious phenomena. It would be listened to, weighed, and perhaps rejected, just like any other news from outside; it would never achieve the privilege of being freed from the coercion of logical thinking. It must first have suffered the fate of repression, the state of being unconscious, before it could produce such mighty effects on its return, and force the masses under its spell, such as we have observed—with astonishment and hitherto without understanding—in religious tradition. And this is a consideration which tilts the balance in favour of the belief that things really happened as I have tried to describe them—or at least very much in that way.

[1] Schiller: *The Gods of Greece* (English translation by E. A. Bowring).

Section II

1. *Summary*

The following part of this essay cannot be sent forth into the world without lengthy explanations and apologies. For it is no other than a faithful, often literal repetition of the first part, save that some of the critical investigations have been condensed and that there are additions referring to the problem of how and why the character of the Jewish people developed in the form it did. I know that this way of presenting my subject is as ineffectual as it is inartistic. I myself disapprove of it wholeheartedly. Why have I not avoided it? The answer to this question is easy for me to find, but rather hard to admit. I have not been able to efface the traces of the unusual way in which this book came to be written.

In truth it has been written twice over. The first time was a few years ago in Vienna, where I did not believe in the possibility of publishing it. I decided to put it away, but it haunted me like an unlaid ghost, and I compromised by publishing two parts of the book independently in the periodical *Imago*. They were the psychoanalytical starting-points of the whole book: "Moses an Egyptian" and the historical essay built on it, "If Moses Was an Egyptian." The rest, which might give offence and was dangerous —namely, the application of my theory to the genesis of monotheism and my interpretation of religion—I kept back, as I thought, for ever. Then in March 1938 came the unexpected German invasion. It forced me to leave my home, but it also freed me of the fear lest my publishing the book might cause psychoanalysis to be forbidden in a country where its practice was still allowed. No sooner had I arrived in England than I found the temptation of making my withheld knowledge accessible to the world irresistible, and so I started to rewrite the third part of my essay, to follow the two already published. This naturally necessitated a re-grouping of the material, if only in part. I did not succeed, however, in fitting in the whole material in this secondary re-editing. On the other hand, I could not make up my mind to relinquish the two former contributions altogether, and that is how the compromise came about of adding unaltered a whole piece of the first version to the second, a device which has the disadvantage of extensive repetition.

I might, it is true, find comfort in the reflection that the matter I treated of was so new and significant —quite apart from whether my presentation of it was correct or not—that it must count as only a minor misfortune if people are made to read about it twice over. There are things that should be said more than once and cannot be repeated often enough. It should, however, be left to the reader's free will whether he wishes to linger with a subject or return to it. A conclusion should not be emphasized by the sly device of dishing up the same subject twice in the same book. By doing so one proves oneself a clumsy writer and has to bear the blame for it. However, the creative power of an author does not, alas, always follow his goodwill. A work grows as it will and sometimes confronts its author as an independent, even an alien creation.

II. *The People of Israel*

If we are quite clear in our minds that a procedure like the present one—to take from the traditional material what seems useful and to reject what is unsuitable, and then to put the individual pieces together according to their psychological probability—does not afford any security for finding the truth, then one is quite right to ask why such an attempt was undertaken. In answer to this I must cite the result. If we substantially reduce the severe demands usually made on a historical and psychological investigation, then it might be possible to clear up problems that have always seemed worthy of attention and that, in consequence of recent events, force themselves again on our observation. We know that of all the peoples who lived in antiquity in the basin of the

Mediterranean the Jewish people is perhaps the only one that still exists in name and probably also in nature. With an unexampled power of resistance it has defied misfortune and ill-treatment, developed special character traits, and, incidentally, earned the hearty dislike of all other peoples. Whence comes this resistance of the Jew and how his character is connected with his fate are things one would like to understand better.

We may start from one character trait of the Jews which governs their relationship to other people. There is no doubt that they have a very good opinion of themselves, think themselves nobler, on a higher level, superior to the others, from whom they are also separated by many of their customs.[1] With this they are animated by a special trust in life, such as is bestowed by the secret possession of a precious gift; it is a kind of optimism. Religious people would call it trust in God.

We know the reason for this attitude of theirs and what their precious treasure is. They really believe themselves to be God's chosen people; they hold themselves to be specially near to him, and this is what makes them proud and confident. According to trustworthy accounts, they behaved in Hellenistic times as they do today. The Jewish character, therefore, even then was what it is now, and the Greeks, among whom and alongside whom they lived, reacted to the Jewish qualities in the same way as their

[1] The insult frequently hurled at them in ancient times that they were lepers (cf. Manetho) must be read as a projection: "They keep apart from us as if we were lepers."

"hosts" do today. They reacted, one might think, as
if they too believed in the preference which the Israelites claimed for themselves. When one is the declared favourite of the dreaded father one need not
be surprised that the other brothers and sisters are
jealous. What this jealousy can lead to is exquisitely
shown in the Jewish legend of Joseph and his breth-
ren. The subsequent course of world history seemed
to justify this Jewish arrogance, for when, later on,
God consented to send mankind a Messiah and Redeemer, he again chose him from among the Jewish
people. The other peoples would then have had reason to say: "Indeed, they were right; they are God's
chosen people." Instead of which it happened that the
salvation through Jesus Christ brought on the Jews
nothing but a stronger hatred, while the Jews themselves derived no advantage from this second proof of
being favoured, because they did not recognize the
Redeemer.

On the strength of my previous remarks we
may say that it was the man Moses who stamped the
Jewish people with this trait, one which became so
significant to them for all time. He enhanced their
self-confidence by assuring them that they were the
chosen people of God; he declared them to be holy
and laid on them the duty to keep apart from others.
Not that the other peoples on their part lacked self-
confidence. Then, just as now, each nation thought
itself superior to all the others. The self-confidence of
the Jews, however, became through Moses anchored
in religion; it became a part of their religious belief.
By the particularly close relationship to their God

they acquired a part of his grandeur. And since we know that behind the God who chose the Jews and delivered them from Egypt stood the man Moses, who achieved that deed, ostensibly at God's command, I venture to say this: it was one man, the man Moses, who created the Jews. To him this people owes its tenacity in supporting life; to him, however, also much of the hostility which it has met with and is meeting still.

III. *The Great Man*

How is it possible that one single man can develop such extraordinary effectiveness, that he can create out of indifferent individuals and families *one* people, can stamp this people with its definite character and determine its fate for millennia to come? Is not such an assumption a retrogression to the manner of thinking that produced creation myths and hero-worship, to times in which historical writing exhausted itself in narrating the dates and life-histories of certain individuals—sovereigns or conquerors? The inclination of modern times tends rather to trace back the events of human history to more hidden, general, and impersonal factors—the forcible influence of economic circumstances, changes in food supply, progress in the use of materials and tools, migrations caused by increase in population and change of climate. In these factors individuals play no other part than that of exponents or representatives of mass tendencies which must come to expression and which found that expression as it were by chance in such persons.

These are quite legitimate points of view, but they remind us of a significant discrepancy between the nature of our thinking-apparatus and the organization of the world which we are trying to apprehend. Our imperative need for cause and effect is satisfied when each process has *one* demonstrable cause. In reality, outside us this is hardly so; each event seems to be over-determined and turns out to be the effect of several converging causes. Intimidated by the countless complications of events, research takes the part of one chain of events against another, stipulates contrasts that do not exist and that are created merely through tearing apart more comprehensive relations.[1]

If, therefore, the investigation of one particular case demonstrates the outstanding influence of a single human personality, our conscience need not reproach us that through accepting this conclusion we have dealt a blow at the doctrine of the significance of those general impersonal factors. In point of fact there is without doubt room for both. In the genesis of monotheism we cannot, it is true, point to any other external factor than those I have already mentioned: namely, that this development has to do with the establishing of closer connections among different nations and the existence of a great empire.

[1] I would guard myself, however, against a possible misunderstanding. I do not mean to say that the world is so complicated that every assertion must hit the truth somewhere. No, our thinking has preserved the liberty of inventing dependencies and connections that have no equivalent in reality. It obviously prizes this gift very highly, since it makes such ample use of it—inside as well as outside of science.

We will keep, therefore, a place for "the great man" in the chain, or rather in the network, of determining causes. It may not be quite useless, however, to ask under what condition we bestow this title of honour. We may be surprised to find that it is not so easy to answer this question. A first formulation which would define as great a human being specially endowed with qualities we value highly is obviously in all respects unsuitable. Beauty, for instance, and muscular strength, much as they may be envied, do not establish a claim to "greatness." There should perhaps be mental qualities present, psychical and intellectual distinction. In the latter respect we have misgivings: a man who has an outstanding knowledge in one particular field would not be called a great man without any further reason. We should certainly not apply the term to a master of chess or to a virtuoso on a musical instrument, and not necessarily to a distinguished artist or a man of science. In such a case we should be content to say he is a great writer, painter, mathematician, or physicist, a pioneer in this field or that, but we should pause before pronouncing him a great man. When we declare, for instance, Goethe, Leonardo da Vinci, and Beethoven to be great men, then something else must move us to do so beyond the admiration of their grandiose creations. If it were not for just such examples one might very well conceive the idea that the title "a great man" is reserved by preference for men of action—that is to say, conquerors, generals, and rulers—and was intended as a recognition of the greatness of their achievements and the strength of the influence that emanated from them. However, this, too, is unsatisfying, and is fully contradicted by our condemnation of so many worthless people of whom one cannot deny that they exercised a great influence on their own and later times. Nor can success be chosen as a distinguishing feature of greatness, if one thinks of the vast number of great men who, instead of being successful, perished after being dogged by misfortune.

We should therefore, tentatively, incline to the conclusion that it is hardly worth while to search for an unequivocal definition of the concept: "a great man." It seems to be a rather loosely used term, one bestowed without due consideration and given to the supernormal development of certain human qualities; in doing so we keep close to the original literal sense of the word "greatness." We may also remember that it is not so much the nature of the great man that arouses our interest as the question of what are the qualities by virtue of which he influences his contemporaries. I propose to shorten this investigation, however, since it threatens to lead us far from our go l.

Let us agree, therefore, that the grea man influences his contemporaries in two way : through his personality and through the idea for which he stands. This idea may lay stress on an old group of wishes in the masses, or point to a new aim for their wishes, or, again, lure the masses by other means. Sometimes—and this is surely the more primitive effect—the personality alone exerts its influence, and the idea plays a decidedly subordinate part. Why the great man should rise to significance at all we have no doubt whatever. We know that the great majority of people have a strong need for authority which they can admire, to which they can submit, and which dominates and sometimes even ill-treats them. We have learned from the psychology of the individual whence comes this need of the masses. It is the longing for the father that lives in each of us from his childhood days, for the same father whom the hero of legend boasts of having overcome. And now it begins to dawn on us that all the features with which we furnish the great man are traits of the father, that in this similarity lies the essence, which so far has eluded us, of the great man. The decisiveness of thought, the strength of will, the forcefulness of his deeds, belong to the picture of the father; above all other things, however, the self-reliance and independence of the great man, his divine conviction of doing the right thing, which may pass into ruthlessness. He must be admired, he may be trusted, but one cannot help also being afraid of him. We should have taken a cue from the word itself; who else but the father should in childhood have been the great man?

Without doubt it must have been a tremendous father imago that stooped in the person of Moses to tell the poor Jewish labourers that they were his dear children. And the conception of a unique, eternal, omnipotent God could not have been less overwhelming for them; he who thought them worthy to make a bond with him promised to take care of them if only they remained faithful to his worship. Probably they did not find it easy to separate the image of the man Moses from that of his God, and their instinct was right in this, since Moses might very well have incorporated into the character of his God some of his own traits, such as his irascibility and implacability. And when they killed this great man they only repeated an evil deed which in primeval times had been a law directed against the divine king, and which, as we know, derives from a still older prototype.[1]

When, on the one hand, the figure of the great man has grown into a divine one, it is time to remember, on the other hand, that the father also was once a child. The great religious idea for which the man Moses stood was, as I have stated, not his own; he had taken it over from his king Ikhnaton. And the latter—whose greatness as a founder of religion is proved without a doubt—perhaps followed intimations which through his mother or by other ways had reached him from the Near or the Far East.

We cannot trace the network any further. If the present argument, however, is correct so far, the idea of monotheism must have returned in the fashion of a boomerang into the country of its origin. It appears fruitless to attempt to ascertain what merit attaches to an individual in a new idea. Obviously many have taken part in its development and made contributions to it. On the other hand it would be wrong to break off the chain of causation with Moses and to neglect what his successors, the Jewish Prophets, achieved. Monotheism had not taken root in Egypt. The same failure might have happened in Israel after the people had thrown off the inconvenient and pretentious religion imposed on them. From the mass of the Jewish people, however, there arose again and

[1] Frazer. Op. cit., p. 192.

again men who lent new colour to the fading tradition, renewed the admonishments and demands of Moses, and did not rest until the lost cause was once more regained. In the constant endeavour of centuries, and last but not least through two great reforms—the one before, the other after the Babylonian exile—there took place the change of the popular God Jahve into the God whose worship Moses had forced upon the Jews. And it is the proof of a special psychical fitness in the mass which had become the Jewish people that it could bring forth so many persons who were ready to take upon themselves the burden of the Mosaic religion for the reward of believing that their people was a chosen one and perhaps for other benefits of a similar order.

iv. *The Progress in Spirituality*

To achieve lasting psychical effects in a people it is obviously not sufficient to assure them that they were specially chosen by God. This assurance must be proved if they are to attach belief to it and draw their conclusions from that belief. In the religion of Moses the Exodus served as such a proof; God, or Moses in his name, did not tire of citing this proof of favour. The feast of the Passover was established to keep this event in mind, or, rather, an old feast was endowed with this memory. Yet it was only a memory. The Exodus itself belonged to a dim past. At the time the signs of God's favour were meagre enough; the fate of the people of Israel would rather indicate his disfavour. Primitive peoples used to depose or even punish their gods if they did not fulfil their duty of granting them victory, fortune, and comfort. Kings have often been treated similarly to gods in every age; the ancient identity of king and god—that is, their common origin—thus becomes manifest. Modern peoples also are in the habit of thus getting rid of their kings if the splendour of their reign is dulled by defeats accompanied by the loss of land and money. Why the people of Israel, however, adhered to their God all the more devotedly the worse they were treated by him—that is a question which we must leave open for the moment.

It may stimulate us to inquire whether the religion of Moses had given the people nothing but an increase in self-confidence through the consciousness of being "chosen." The next element is indeed easily found. Their religion also gave to the Jews a much more grandiose idea of their God or, to express it more soberly, the idea of a more august God. Whoever believed in this God took part in his greatness, so to speak, might feel uplifted himself. This may not be quite obvious to unbelievers, but it may be illustrated by the simile of the high confidence a Briton would feel in a foreign land made unsafe by revolt, a confidence in which a subject of some small Continental state would be entirely lacking. The Briton counts on his government to send a warship if a hair of his head is touched, and also on the rebels' knowing very well that this is so, while the small state does not even own a warship. The pride in the greatness of the British Empire has therefore one of its

roots in the consciousness of the greater security and
protection that a British subject enjoys. The same
may be true of the idea of the great God, and—since
one would hardly presume to assist God in his con-
duct of the world—pride in the greatness of God goes
together with that of being "chosen."

Among the precepts of Mosaic religion is one
that has more significance than is at first obvious. It
is the prohibition against making an image of God,
which means the compulsion to worship an invisible
God. I surmise that in this point Moses surpassed the
Aton religion in strictness. Perhaps he meant to be
consistent; his God was to have neither a name nor
a countenance. The prohibition was perhaps a fresh
precaution against magic malpractices. If this prohibition was accepted, however, it was bound to exercise
a profound influence. For it signified subordinating
sense perception to an abstract idea; it was a triumph
of spirituality over the senses; more precisely, an
instinctual renunciation[1] accompanied by its psychologically necessary consequences.

To make more credible what at first glance
does not appear convincing we must call to mind
other processes of similar character in the development of human culture. The earliest among them,
and perhaps the most important, we can discern only
in dim outline in the obscurity of primeval times. Its
surprising effects make it necessary to conclude that it
happened. In our children, in adult neurotics, as well
as in primitive people, we find the mental phenome-

[1] I use this phrase (*Triebverzicht*) as an abbreviation for
"renouncing the satisfaction of an urge derived from an instinct."
—*Translator*.

non which I have called the belief in the "omnipotence of thoughts." We judge it to be an over-estimation of the influence which our mental faculties
—the intellectual ones in this case—can exert on the
outer world by changing it. All magic, the predecessor
of science, is basically founded on these premisses. All
magic of words belongs here, as does the conviction
of the power connected with the knowledge and the
pronouncing of a name. We surmise that "omnipotence of thoughts" was the expression of the pride
mankind took in the development of language, which
had brought in its train such an extraordinary increase in the intellectual faculties. There opened then
the new realm of spirituality where conceptions, memories, and deductions became of decisive importance,
in contrast to the lower psychical activity which concerned itself with the immediate perceptions of the
sense organs. It was certainly one of the most important stages on the way to becoming human.

Another process of later time confronts us in a
much more tangible form. Under the influence of external conditions—which we need not follow up here
and which in part are also not sufficiently known—
it happened that the matriarchal structure of society
was replaced by a patriarchal one. This naturally
brought with it a revolution in the existing state of
the law. An echo of this revolution can still be heard,
I think, in the *Oresteia* of Æschylus. This turning
from the mother to the father, however, signifies above
all a victory of spirituality over the senses—that is to
say, a step forward in culture, since maternity is
proved by the senses whereas paternity is a surmise

based on a deduction and a premiss. This declaration in favour of the thought-process, thereby raising it above sense perception, was proved to be a step charged with serious consequences.

Some time between the two cases I have mentioned, another event took place which shows a closer relationship to the ones we have investigated in the history of religion. Man found that he was faced with the acceptance of "spiritual" forces—that is to say, such forces as cannot be apprehended by the senses, particularly not by sight, and yet having undoubted, even extremely strong effects. If we may trust to language, it was the movement of the air that provided the image of spirituality, since the spirit borrows its name from the breath of wind (*animus, spiritus,* Hebrew *ruach* = smoke). The idea of the soul was thus born as the spiritual principle in the individual. Observation found the breath of air again in the human breath, which ceases with death; even today we talk of a dying man breathing his last. Now the realm of spirits had opened for man, and he was ready to endow everything in nature with the soul he had discovered in himself. The whole world became animated, and science, coming so much later, had enough to do in disestablishing the former state of affairs and has not yet finished this task.

Through the Mosaic prohibition, God was raised to a higher level of spirituality; the door was opened to further changes in the idea of God, of which I shall speak later. At present another of its effects will occupy us. All such progress in spirituality results in increasing self-confidence, in making people proud so that they feel superior to those who have remained in the bondage of the senses. We know that Moses had given the Jews the proud feeling óf being God's chosen people; by dematerializing God a new, valuable contribution was made to the secret treasure of the people. The Jews preserved their inclination towards spiritual interests. The political misfortune of the nation taught them to appreciate the only possession they had retained, their written records, at its true value. Immediately after the destruction of the Temple in Jerusalem by Titus, Rabbi Jochanan ben Sakkai asked for permission to open at Jabneh the first school for the study of the Torah. From now on, it was the Holy Book, and the study of it, that kept the scattered people together.

So much is generally known and accepted. I only wished to add that this whole development, so characteristic of the Jews, had been initiated by Moses' prohibition against worshipping God in a visible form.

The preference which through two thousand years the Jews have given to spiritual endeavour has, of course, had its effect; it has helped to build a dike against brutality and the inclination to violence which are usually found where athletic development becomes the ideal of the people. The harmonious development of spiritual and bodily activity, as achieved by the Greeks, was denied to the Jews. In this conflict their decision was at least made in favour of what is culturally the more important.

v. *Renunciation versus Gratification*[1]

It is not at all obvious why progress in spirituality and subordination of the senses should raise the self-confidence of a person as well as of a nation. This seems to presuppose a definite standard of value and another person or institution who uses it. For an explanation we turn to an analogous case in the psychology of the individual, which we have learned to understand.

When the Id makes an instinctual demand of an erotic or aggressive nature on a human being, the most simple and natural response for the Ego, which governs the apparatus for thinking and muscle innervation, is to satisfy this by an action. This satisfaction of the instinct is felt as pleasure by the Ego, just as not satisfying this instinct would undoubtedly become a source of discomfort. Now, it may happen that the Ego eschews satisfaction of the instinct because of external obstacles—namely, when it realizes that the action in question would bring in its course serious danger to the Ego. Such a refraining from satisfaction, an "instinctual renunciation" because of external obstacles—as we say, in obedience to the reality-principle—is never pleasurable. The instinctual renunciation would bring about a lasting painful tension if we did not succeed in diminishing the strength of the instinctual urge itself through a displacement of energy. This instinctual renunciation

[1] See footnote on p. 144.—*Translator*.

may also be forced on us, however, by other motives, which we rightly call inner ones. In the course of individual development a part of the inhibiting forces in the outer world becomes internalized; a standard is created in the Ego which opposes the other faculties by observation, criticism, and prohibition. We call this new standard the *Super-ego*. From now on, the Ego, before undertaking to satisfy the instincts, has to consider not only the dangers of the outer world, but also the objections of the Super-ego, and has therefore more occasion for refraining from satisfying the instinct. While, however, instinctual renunciation for external reasons is only painful, renunciation for internal reasons, in obedience to the demands of the Super-ego, has another economic effect. It brings besides the inevitable pain a gain in pleasure to the Ego—as it were, a substitutive satisfaction. The Ego feels uplifted; it is proud of the renunciation as of a valuable achievement. We think we can follow the mechanism of this gain in pleasure. The Super-ego is the successor and representative of the parents (and educators) who superintended the actions of the individual in his first years of life; it perpetuates their functions almost without a change. It keeps the Ego in lasting dependence and exercises a steady pressure. The Ego is concerned, just as it was in childhood, to retain the love of its master, and it feels his appreciation as a relief and satisfaction, his reproaches as pricks of conscience. When the Ego has made the sacrifice to the Super-ego of renouncing an instinctual satisfaction, it expects to be rewarded by being loved all the more. The consciousness of deserving this love is felt as pride. At a time when the authority was not yet internalized as Super-ego the relation between the threatened loss of love and the instinctual demand would have been the same. A feeling of security and satisfaction results if out of love to one's parents one achieves an instinctual renunciation. This good feeling could acquire the peculiar narcissistic character of pride only after the authority itself had become a part of the Ego.

How does this explanation of gaining satisfaction through instinctual renunciation help us in understanding the process we wish to study—namely, the increase of self-confidence that accompanies progress in spirituality? Apparently they help very little, for the circumstances here are very different. There is no instinctual enunciation, and there is no second person or higher standard for whose benefit the sacrifice is made. The second statement will soon appear doubtful. One might say that the great man is the authority for whose sake the effort is made, and since the great man achieves this because he is a father substitute we need not be surprised if he is allotted the role of Super-ego in mass psychology. This would, therefore, hold good for the man Moses in his relationship to the Jewish people. In other points, however, there would seem to be no proper analogy. The progress in spirituality consists in deciding against the direct sense perception in favour of the so-called higher intellectual processes—that is to say, in favour of memories, reflection, and deduction. An example of this would be the decision that paternity is more important than maternity, although the former cannot be proved by the senses as the latter can. This is why the child has to have the father's name and inherit after him. Another example would be: our God is the greatest and mightiest, although he is invisible like the storm and the soul. Rejecting a sexual or aggressive instinctual demand seems to be something very different from this. In many examples of progress in spirituality—for instance, in the triumph of father-right—we cannot point to the authority that provides the measure for what is to be valued the more highly. In this case it cannot be the father himself, since it is only this progress that raises him to the rank of an authority. We are therefore confronted with the phenomenon that during the development of mankind the world of the senses becomes gradually mastered by spirituality, and that man feels proud and uplifted by each such step in progress. One does not know, however, why this should be so. Still later it happens that spirituality itself is overpowered by the altogether mysterious emotional phenomenon of belief. This is the famous *credo quia absurdum*, and whoever has compassed this regards it as the highest achievement. Perhaps what is common to all these psychological situations is something else. Perhaps man declares simply that the higher achievement is what is more difficult to attain, and his pride in it is only narcissism heightened by his consciousness of having overcome difficulty.

These considerations are certainly not very fruitful, and one might think that they have nothing to do with our investigation into what determined the character of the Jewish people. This would be only to our advantage, but that this train of thought has all the same to do with our problem is shown by a fact that will occupy us later more extensively. The religion that began with the prohibition against making an image of its God has developed in the course of centuries more and more into a religion of instinctual renunciation. Not that it demands sexual abstinence; it is content with a considerable restriction of sexual freedom. God, however, becomes completely withdrawn from sexuality and raised to an ideal of ethical perfection. Ethics, however, means restriction of instinctual gratification. The Prophets did not tire of maintaining that God demands nothing else from his people but a just and virtuous life—that is to say, abstention from the gratification of all impulses that, according to our present-day moral standards, are to be condemned as vicious. And even the exhortation to believe in God seems to recede in comparison with the seriousness of these ethical demands. Instinctual renunciation thus appears to play a prominent part in religion, although it had not been present in it from the beginning.

Here is the place to make a statement which should obviate a misunderstanding. Though it may seem that instinctual renunciation, and the ethics based on it, do not belong to the essence of religion, still they are genetically closely related to religion. Totemism, the first form of religion of which we know, contains as an indispensable part of its system a number of laws and prohibitions which plainly mean nothing else but instinctual renunciation. There is the worship of the totem, which contains the prohibition against killing or harming it; exogamy (that is to say, the renunciation of the passionately desired mothers and sisters of the horde); the granting of equal rights to all members of the brother horde (that is, the restriction of the impulse to settle their rivalry by brute force). In these rules we have to discern the first beginnings of a moral and social order. It does not escape our notice that here two different motivations come into play. The first two prohibitions work in the direction of what the murdered father would have wished; they, so to speak, perpetuate his will. The third law, the one giving equal rights to the brothers, ignores the father's wishes. Its sense lies in the need of preserving permanently the new order which was established after the death of the father. Otherwise reversion to the former state would have been inevitable. Here social laws became separated from others which, we might say, originated directly from a religious context.

In the abbreviated development of the human individual the most important events of that process are repeated. Here also it is the parents' authority— essentially that of the all-powerful father, who wields the power of punishment—that demands instinctual renunciation on the part of the child and determines what is allowed and what is forbidden. What the child calls "good" or "naughty" becomes later, when society and Super-ego take the place of the parents, "good," in the sense of moral, or "evil," virtuous or vicious. But it is still the same thing: instinctual renunciation through the presence of the authority which replaced and continued that of the father.

Our insight into these problems becomes further deepened when we investigate the strange conception of sanctity. What is it really that appears "sacred" compared with other things which we respect highly and admit to be important and significant? On the one hand the connection between the sacred and the religious is unmistakable; it is so stressed as to be obvious. Everything connected with religion is sacred; it is the very core of sanctity. On the other hand our judgment is disturbed by the numerous attempts to lay claim to the character of holiness by so many other things—persons, institutions, and procedures that have little to do with religion. These endeavours are often plainly tendentious. Let us proceed from the feature of prohibition which adheres so closely to religion. The sacred is obviously something that must not be touched. A sacred prohibition has a very strong affective note, but actually it has no rational motivation. For why should it be such a specially hideous crime to commit incest with a daughter or sister, so much more so than any other sexual relations? When we ask for an explanation we shall surely be told that all our feelings cry out against such a crime. Yet all this means is that the prohibition is taken to be self-evident, that we do not know how to explain it.

That such an explanation is illusory can easily be proved. What is reputed to offend our feelings used to be a general custom—one might say, a sacred tradition—in the ruling families of the ancient Egyptians and other peoples. It went without saying that each Pharaoh found his first and foremost wife in his sister, and the successors of the Pharaohs, the Greek Ptolemies, did not hesitate to follow this example. So far we seem to discern that incest—in this case between brother and sister—was a prerogative forbidden to ordinary mortals and reserved for kings who represented the gods on earth. The world of the Greek and Germanic myths also took no exception to these incestuous relationships. We may surmise that the anxious concern for "family" in our higher nobility is a remnant of that old privilege, and we observe that, as a consequence of inbreeding continued through many generations in the highest social circles, the crowned heads of Europe today consist in effect of one family.

To point to the incest of gods, kings, and heroes helps to dispose of another attempt at explanation— namely, the one that would explain the horror of incest biologically and reduce it to an instinctive knowledge of the harmfulness of inbreeding. It is not even certain, however, that there lies any danger in inbreeding, let alone that primitive races recognized it and guarded against it. The uncertainty in determining permitted and prohibited relationships is another argument against presupposing a "natural feeling" as an original motive for the horror of incest.

Our reconstruction of prehistory forces another explanation on us. The law of exogamy, the negative expression of which is the fear of incest, was the will of the father and continued it after his murder. Hence the strength of its affectivity and the impossibility of a rational motivation—in short, its sacredness. I should confidently anticipate that an investigation of all other cases of sacred prohibitions would lead to the same result as that of the horror of incest—namely, that what is sacred was originally nothing but the perpetuated will of the primeval father. This would also elucidate the ambivalence of the word, hitherto inexplicable, which expresses the conception of sacredness. It is the ambivalence which governs the relationship to the father. *"Sacer"* does not only mean "sacred," "blessed," but also something that we can only translate by "accursed," "worthy of disgust" (*"auri sacra fames"*). The will of the father, however, was not only something which one must not touch, which one had to hold in high honour, but also something which made one shudder because it necessitated a painful instinctual renunciation. When we hear that Moses "sanctified" his people by introducing the custom of circumcision, we now understand the deep-lying meaning of this pretension. Circumcision is the symbolical substitute of castration, a punishment which the primeval father dealt his sons long ago out of the fullness of his power; and whosoever accepted this symbol showed by so doing that he was ready to submit to the father's will, although it was at the cost of a painful sacrifice.

To return to ethics: we may say in conclusion that a part of its precepts is explained rationally by the necessity of marking off the rights of the community to the individual, those of the individual to the community, and those of individuals to one another. What, however, appears mysterious, grandiose, and mystically self-evident owes its character to its connection with religion, its origin in the will of the father.

VI. *The Truth in Religion*

How we who have little belief envy those who are convinced of the existence of a Supreme Power, for whom the world holds no problems because he himself has created all its institutions! How comprehensive, exhaustive, and final are the doctrines of the believers compared with the laboured, poor, and patchy attempts at explanation which are the best we can produce! The Divine Spirit, which in itself is the ideal of ethical perfection, has planted within the soul of men the knowledge of this ideal and at the same time the urge to strive towards it. They feel immediately what is high and noble and what low and mean. Their emotional life is measured by the distance from their ideal. It affords them high gratification when they—in perihelion, so to speak—come nearer to it; and they are punished by severe distress when—in aphelion—they have moved farther away from it. All this is so simply and unshakably established. We can only regret it if certain experiences of life and observations of nature have made it impossible to accept the hypothesis of such a Supreme Being. As if the world had not enough problems, we are confronted with the task of finding out how those who have faith in a Divine Being could have acquired it, and whence this belief derives the enormous power that enables it to overwhelm Reason and Science.[1]

An allusion to the passage in *Faust:* "*Verachte nur Vernunft und Wissenschaft.*"—*Translator.*

Let us return to the more modest problem that has occupied us so far. We set out to explain whence comes the peculiar character of the Jewish people which in all probability is what has enabled that people to survive until today. We found that the man Moses created their character by giving to them a religion which heightened their self-confidence to such a degree that they believed themselves to be superior to all other peoples. They survived by keeping aloof from the others. Admixture of blood made little difference, since what kept them together was something ideal—the possession they had in common of certain intellectual and emotional values. The Mosaic religion had this effect (1) because it allowed the people to share in the grandeur of its new conception of God, (2) because it maintained that the people had been "chosen" by this great God and was destined to enjoy the proofs of his special favour, and (3) because it forced upon the people a progress in spirituality which, significant enough in itself, further opened the way to respect for intellectual work and to further instinctual renunciations.

This, then, is the conclusion we have attained, but although I do not wish to retract anything I have said before, I cannot help feeling that it is somehow not altogether satisfactory. The cause does not, so to speak, accord with the result. The fact we are trying to explain seems to be incommensurate with everything we adduce by way of explanation. Is it possible that all our investigations have so far discovered not the whole motivation, but only a superficial layer, and that behind this lies hidden another very significant component? Considering how extraordinarily complicated all causation in life and history is, we should have been prepared for something of that kind.

The path to this deeper motivation starts at a certain passage in the previous discussion. The religion of Moses did not achieve its effects immediately, but in a strangely indirect manner. This does not mean that it did not itself produce the effect. It took a long time, many centuries, to do so; that goes without saying where the development of a people's character is concerned. Our modification, however, refers to a fact which we have taken from the history of Jewish religion or, if one prefers, introduced into it. I said that the Jewish people shook off the religion of Moses after a certain time; whether they did so completely or whether they retained some of its precepts we cannot tell. In accepting the supposition that during the long period of the fight for Canaan, and the struggles with the peoples settled there, the Jahve religion did not substantially differ from the worship of the other Baalim, we stand on historical ground, in spite of all the later tendentious attempts to obscure this shaming state of affairs. The religion of Moses, however, had not perished. A sort of memory of it had survived, obscured and distorted, but perhaps supported by individual members of the priest caste through the ancient scripts. It was this tradition of a great past that continued to exert its effect from the background; it slowly attained more and more power over the minds of the people, and at last succeeded in changing the God Jahve into the God of Moses and in bringing again to life the abandoned religion Moses had instituted centuries before.

Earlier in this book[1] I have discussed the hypothesis that would seem to be inevitable if we are to find comprehensible such an achievement on the part of tradition.

VII. *The Return of the Repressed*

There are a number of similar processes among those which the analytic investigation of mental life has made known to us. Some of them are termed pathological; others are counted among the varieties of the normal. This matters little, however, for the limits between the two are not strictly defined, and the mechanisms are to a certain extent the same. It is much more important whether the changes in question take place in the Ego itself or whether they confront it as alien; in the latter case they are called symptoms. From the fullness of the material at my disposal I will choose cases that concern the formation of character.

A young girl had developed into the most decided contrast to her mother; she had cultivated all the qualities she missed in her mother and avoided all those that reminded her of her mother. I may add that in former years she had identified herself with her mother—like any other female child—and had now come to oppose this identification energetically.

[1] Cf. pp. 87–90.

When this girl married, however, and became a wife and mother in her turn, we are surprised to find that she became more and more like the mother towards whom she felt so inimical, until at last the mother-identification she had overcome had once more unmistakably won the day. The same thing happens with boys, and even the great Goethe, who in his *Sturm und Drang* period certainly did not respect his pedantic and stiff father very highly, developed in old age traits that belonged to his father's character. This result will stand out more strikingly where the contrast between the two persons is more pronounced. A young man, whose fate was determined by his having to grow up with a good-for-nothing father, developed at first—in spite of the father—into a capable, trustworthy, and honourable man. In the prime of life his character changed and from then on he behaved as if he had taken this same father as his example. So as not to lose the connection with our topic we must keep in mind that at the beginning of such a process there always exists an identification with the father from early childhood days. This gets repudiated, even over-compensated, and in the end again comes to light.

It has long since become common knowledge, that the experience of the first five years of childhood exert a decisive influence on our life, one which later events oppose in vain. Much could be said about how these early experiences resist all efforts of more mature years to modify them, but this would not be relevant. It may not be so well known, however, that the strongest obsessive influence derives from those experiences which the child undergoes at a time when we have reason to believe his psychical apparatus to be incompletely fitted for accepting them. The fact itself cannot be doubted, but it seems so strange that we might try to make it easier to understand by a simile; the process may be compared to a photograph, which can be developed and made into a picture after a short or long interval. Here I may point out, however, that an imaginative writer, with the boldness permitted to such writers, made this disconcerting discovery before me. E. T. A. Hoffmann used to explain the wealth of imaginative figures that offered themselves to him for his stories by the quickly changing pictures and impressions he had received during a journey in a post-chaise, lasting for several weeks, while he was still a babe at his mother's breast. What a child has experienced and not understood by the time he has reached the age of two he may never again remember, except in his dreams. Only through psychoanalytic treatment will he become aware of those events. At any time in later years, however, they may break into his life with obsessive impulsiveness, direct his actions, force him to like or dislike people, and often decide the choice of his love-object by a preference that so often cannot be rationally defended. The two points that touch on our problem are unmistakable. They are, first, the remoteness of time,[1]

[1] Here also a poet may speak for us. To explain his attachment he imagines:

> *Ach, du warst in abgelebten Zeiten*
> *Meine Schwester oder meine Frau.*
>
> (For in previous lives we both have passed through
> You, Love, were my sister or my wife.)
> Goethe, Vol. IV of the Weimar edition, p. 97.

which is considered here as the really decisive factor, as, for instance, in the special state of memory that in these childhood experiences we class as "unconscious." In this feature we expect to find an analogy with the state of mind that we ascribe to tradition when it is active in the mental emotional life of a people. It was not easy, it is true, to introduce the conception of the unconscious into mass psychology.

Contributions to the phenomena we are looking for are regularly made by the mechanisms that lead to a neurosis. Here also the decisive experiences in early childhood exert a lasting influence, yet in this case the stress falls not on the time, but on the process opposing that event, the reaction against it. Schematically expressed, it is thus: As a consequence of a certain experience there arises an instinctual demand which claims satisfaction. The Ego forgoes this satisfaction, either because it is paralysed by the excessiveness of the demand or because it recognizes in it a danger. The first of these reasons is the original one; both end in the avoidance of a dangerous situation. The Ego guards against this danger by repression. The excitation becomes inhibited in one way or another; the incitement, with the observations and perceptions belonging to it, is forgotten. This, however, does not bring the process to an end; either the instinct has kept its strength, or it will regain it, or it is reawakened by a new situation. It renews its claim and—since the way to normal satisfaction is barred by what we may call the scar tissue of repression—it gains at some weak point new access to a so-called substitutive satisfaction which now appears as a symptom, without the acquiescence and also without the comprehension of the Ego. All phenomena of symptom-formation can be fairly described as "the return of the repressed." The distinctive character of them, however, lies in the extensive distortion the returning elements have undergone, compared with their original form. Perhaps the objection will be raised here that in this last group of facts I have deviated too much from the similarity with tradition. I shall feel no regret, however, if this has led us nearer to the problems of instinctual renunciation.

VIII. *The Historical Truth*

I have made all these psychological digressions to make it more credible that the religion of Moses exercised influence on the Jewish people only when it had become a tradition. We have scarcely achieved more than a probability. Yet let us assume we have succeeded in proving this conclusively; the impression would still remain that we had satisfied only the qualitative factor of our task, not the quantitative as well. To all matters concerning the creation of a religion—and certainly to that of the Jewish one—pertains something majestic, which has not so far been covered by our explanations. Some other element should have part in it: one that has few analogies and nothing quite like it, something unique and commensurate with that which has grown out of it, something like religion itself.

Let us see if we can approach our subject from

the reverse side. We understand that primitive man needs a god as creator of the world, as head of his tribe, and as one who takes care of him. This god takes his place behind the dead fathers of whom tradition still has something to relate. Man in later times—in our time, for instance—behaves similarly. He also remains infantile and needs protection, even when he is fully grown; he feels he cannot relinquish the support of his god. So much is indisputable, but it is not so easily to be understood why there must be only one god, why just the progress from henotheism to monotheism acquires such an overwhelming significance. It is true, as I have mentioned before, that the believer participates in the greatness of his god, and the more powerful the god, the surer the protection he can bestow. The power of a god, however, need not presuppose his being an only god: many peoples only glorified their chief god the more if he ruled over a multitude of inferior gods; he was not the less great because there were other gods than he. It also meant sacrificing some of the intimate relationship if the god became universal and cared equally for all lands and peoples. One had, so to speak, to share one's god with strangers and had to compensate oneself for that by believing that one was favoured by him. The point could be made that the conception of an Only God signifies a step forward in spirituality; this point, however, cannot be estimated so very highly.

The true believer knows of a way adequately to fill in this obvious gap in motivation. He says that the idea of an Only God has had this overwhelming effect on mankind because it is part of eternal truth, which, hidden for so long, has at last come to light and has swept all before it. We have to admit that at last we have an element of an order commensurate to the greatness of the subject as well as to that of the success of its influence.

I also should like to accept this solution. However, I have my misgivings. The religious argument is based on an optimistic and idealistic premiss. The human intellect has not shown itself elsewhere to be endowed with a very good scent for truth, nor has the human mind displayed any special readiness to accept truth On the contrary, it is the general experience that the human intellect errs very easily without our suspecting it at all, and that nothing is more readily believed than what—regardless of the truth—meets our wishes and illusions half-way. That is why our agreement needs modifying. I too should credit the believer's solution with containing the truth; it is not, however, the material truth, but a historical truth. I would claim the right to correct a certain distortion which this truth underwent on its re-emergence. That is to say, I do not believe that one supreme great God "exists" today, but I believe that in primeval times there was one person who must needs appear gigantic and who, raised to the status of a deity, returned to the memory of men.

Our supposition was that the religion of Moses was discarded and partly forgotten and that, later on, it forced itself on the notice of the people as a tradition. I make the assumption that this process was the repetition of an earlier one. When Moses gave to his people the conception of an Only God it was not an altogether new idea, for it meant the reanimation of primeval experience in the human family that had long ago faded from the conscious memory of mankind. The experience was such an important one, however, and had produced, or at least prepared, such far-reaching changes in the life of man that, I cannot help thinking, it must have left some permanent trace in the human soul—something comparable to a tradition.

The psychoanalyses of individuals have taught us that their earliest impressions, received at a time when they were hardly able to talk, manifest themselves later in an obsessive fashion, although those impressions themselves are not consciously remembered. We feel that the same must hold good for the earliest experiences of mankind. One result of this is the emergence of the conception of one great God. It must be recognized as a memory—a distorted one, it is true, but nevertheless a memory. It has an obsessive quality; it simply must be believed. As far as its distortion goes, it may be called a delusion; in so far as it brings to light something from the past, it must be called truth. The psychiatric delusion also contains a particle of truth; the patient's conviction issues from this and extends to the whole delusional fabrication surrounding it.

The following pages contain a scarcely altered repetition of what I said in the first section. In 1912 I tried in my book *Totem and Taboo* to reconstruct the ancient situation from which all these effects issued. In that book I made use of certain theoretical reflections of Charles Darwin, J. J. Atkinson, and especially

Robertson Smith, and combined them with findings and suggestions from psychoanalytic practice. From Darwin I borrowed the hypothesis that men originally lived in small hordes; each of the hordes stood under the rule of an older male, who governed by brute force, appropriated all the females, and belaboured or killed all the young males, including his own sons. From Atkinson I received the suggestion that this patriarchal system came to an end through a rebellion of the sons, who united against the father, overpowered him, and together consumed his body. Following Robertson Smith's totem theory, I suggested that this horde, previously ruled by the father, was followed by a totemistic brother clan. In order to be able to live in peace with one another the victorious brothers renounced the women for whose sake they had killed the father, and agreed to practise exogamy. The power of the father was broken and the families were regulated by matriarchy. The ambivalence of the sons towards the father remained in force during the whole further development. Instead of the father a certain animal was declared the totem; it stood for their ancestor and protecting spirit, and no one was allowed to hurt or kill it. Once a year, however, the whole clan assembled for a feast at which the otherwise revered totem was torn to pieces and eaten. No one was permitted to abstain from this feast; it was the solemn repetition of the father-murder, in which social order, moral laws, and religion had had their beginnings. The correspondence of the totem feast (according to Robertson Smith's description) with the

Christian Communion has struck many authors before me.

I still adhere to this sequence of thought. I have often been vehemently reproached for not changing my opinions in later editions of my book, since more recent ethnologists have without exception discarded Robertson Smith's theories and have in part replaced them by others which differ extensively. I would reply that these alleged advances in science are well known to me. Yet I have not been convinced either of their correctness or of Robertson Smith's errors. Contradiction is not always refutation; a new theory does not necessarily denote progress. Above all, however, I am not an ethnologist, but a psychoanalyst. It was my good right to select from ethnological data what would serve me for my analytic work. The writings of the highly gifted Robertson Smith provided me with valuable points of contact with the psychological material of analysis and suggestions for the use of it. I cannot say the same of the work of his opponents.

IX. *The Historical Development*

I cannot reproduce here the contents of *Totem and Taboo*, but I must try to account for the long interval that took place between the events which I suggested happened in primeval times and the victory of monotheism in historical times. After the combination of brother clan, matriarchy, exogamy, and totem-

ism had been established there began a development
which may be described as a slow "return of the repressed." The term "repressed" is here used not in its
technical sense. Here I mean something past, vanished,
and overcome in the life of a people, which I venture
to treat as equivalent to repressed material in the
mental life of the individual. In what psychological
form the past existed during its period of darkness we
cannot as yet tell. It is not easy to translate the con-
cepts of individual psychology into mass psychology,
and I do not think that much is to be gained by introducing the concept of a "collective" unconscious—the
content of the unconscious is collective anyhow, a
general possession of mankind. So in the meantime
the use of analogies must help us out. The processes
we study here in the life of a people are very similar
to those we know from psychopathology, but still they
are not quite the same. We must conclude that the
mental residue of those primeval times has become a
heritage which, with each new generation, needs only
to be awakened, not to be reacquired. We may think
here of the example of speech symbolism, which certainly seems to be inborn. It originates in the time of
speech-development, and it is familiar to all children
without their having been specially instructed. It is the
same in all peoples in spite of the differences in language. What we may still lack in certainty we may
acquire from other results of psychoanalytic investigations. We learn that our children in a number of
significant relationships do not react as their own
experiences would lead us to expect, but instinctively,

like animals; this is explicable only by phylogenetic inheritance.

The return of the repressed proceeds slowly; it certainly does not occur spontaneously, but under the influence of all the changes in the conditions of life that abound throughout the history of civilization. I can give here neither a survey of the conditions on which it depends nor any more than a scanty enumeration of the stages in which the return proceeds. The father became again the head of the family, but he was no longer omnipotent as the father of the primeval horde had been. In clearly recognizable transitional stages the totem animal was ousted by the god. The god, in human form, still carried at first the head of an animal; later on he was wont to assume the guise of the same animal. Still later the animal became sacred to him and his favourite companion or else he was reputed to have slain the animal, when he added its name to his own. Between the totem animal and the god the hero made his appearance; this was often an early stage of deification. The idea of a Highest Being seems to have appeared early; at first it was shadowy and devoid of any connection with the daily interests of mankind. As the tribes and peoples were knit together into larger unities, the gods also became organized into families and hierarchies. Often one of them was elevated to be the overlord of gods and men. The next step, to worship only one god, was taken hesitatingly, and at long last the decision was made to concede all power to one God only and not to suffer any other gods beside him. Only then was the grandeur of the primeval father restored; the emotions belonging to him could now be repeated.

The first effect of the reunion with what men had long missed and yearned for was overwhelming and exactly as the tradition of the law-giving on Mount Sinai depicts it. There was admiration, awe, and gratitude that the people had found favour in his eyes; the religion of Moses knows of only these positive feelings towards the Father God The conviction that his power was irresistible, the subjection to his will, could not have been more absolute with the helpless, intimidated son of the father of the horde than they were here; indeed, they become fully comprehensible only by transformation into the primitive and infantile milieu. Infantile feelings are far more intense and inexhaustibly deep than are those of adults; only religious ecstasy can bring back that intensity. Thus a transport of devotion to God is the first response to the return of the Great Father.

The direction of this Father religion was thus fixed for all time, but its development was not thereby finished. Ambivalency belongs to the essence of the father-son relationship; it had to happen that in the course of time the hostility should be stirred up which in ancient times had spurred the sons to slay their admired and dreaded father. In the religion of Moses itself there was no room for direct expression of the murderous father-hate. Only a powerful reaction to it could make its appearance: the consciousness of guilt because of that hostility, the bad conscience because one had sinned against God and continued so to sin. This feeling of guiltiness, which the Prophets incessantly kept alive and which soon became an integral part of the religious system itself, had another, superficial motivation which cleverly veiled the true origin of the feeling. The people met with hard times; the hopes based on the favour of God were slow in being fulfilled; it became not easy to adhere to the illusion, cherished above all else, that they were God's chosen people. If they wished to keep happiness, then the consciousness of guilt because they themselves were such sinners offered a welcome excuse for God's severity. They deserved nothing better than to be punished by him, because they did not observe the laws; the need for satisfying this feeling of guilt, which, coming from a much deeper source, was insatiable, made them render their religious precepts ever and ever more strict, more exacting, but also more petty. In a new transport of moral asceticism the Jews imposed on themselves constantly increasing instinctual renunciation, and thereby reached—at least in doctrine and precepts—ethical heights that had remained inaccessible to the other peoples of antiquity. Many Jews regard these aspirations as the second main characteristic, and the second great achievement, of their religion. Our investigation is intended to show how it is connected with the first one, the conception of the one and only God. The origin, however, of this ethics in feelings of guilt, due to the repressed hostility to God, cannot be gainsaid. It bears the characteristic of being never concluded and never able to be concluded with which we are familiar in the reactionformations of obsessional neurosis.

The further development transcends Judaism.

Other elements re-emerging from the drama enacted around the person of the primeval father were in no way to be reconciled with the Mosaic religion. The consciousness of guilt in that epoch was no longer restricted to the Jews; it had seized all Mediterranean peoples as a vague discomfort, a premonition of misfortune, the reason for which no one knew. Modern history speaks of the ageing of antique culture. I would surmise that it has apprehended only some of the casual and adjuvant causes for the mood of dejection then prevailing among the peoples. The lightening of that oppression proceeded from the Jews. Although food for the idea had been provided by many suggestive hints from various quarters, it was, nevertheless, in the mind of a Jew, Saul of Tarsus, who as a Roman citizen was called Paul, that the perception dawned: "It is because we killed God the Father that we are so unhappy." It is quite clear to us now why he could grasp this truth in no other form but in the delusional guise of the glad tidings: "We have been delivered from all guilt since one of us laid down his life to expiate our guilt." In this formulation the murder of God was, of course, not mentioned, but a crime that had to be expiated by a sacrificial death could only have been murder. Further, the connection between the delusion and the historical truth was established by the assurance that the sacrificial victim was the Son of God. The strength which this new faith derived from its source in historical truth enabled it to overcome all obstacles; in the place of the enrapturing feeling of being the chosen ones, there came now release through salvation. The

fact of the father-murder, however, had on its return
to the memory of mankind to overcome greater obstacles than the one which constituted the essence of
monotheism; it had to undergo a more extensive distortion. The unmentionable crime was replaced by
the tenet of the somewhat shadowy conception of
original sin.

Original sin and salvation through sacrificial
death became the basis of the new religion founded by
Paul. The question whether there was a leader and
instigator to the murder among the horde of brothers
who rebelled against the primeval father, or whether
that figure was created later by poets who identified
themselves with the hero and was then incorporated
into tradition, must remain unanswered. After the
Christian doctrine had burst the confines of Judaism,
it absorbed constituents from many other sources, renounced many features of pure monotheism, and
adopted in many particulars the ritual of the other
Mediterranean peoples. It was as if Egypt had come to
wreak her vengeance on the heirs of Ikhnaton. The
way in which the new religion came to terms with
the ancient ambivalency in the father-son relationship
is noteworthy. Its main doctrine, to be sure, was the
reconciliation with God the Father, the expiation of
the crime committed against him; but the other side
of the relationship manifested itself in the Son, who
had taken the guilt on his shoulders, becoming God
himself beside the Father and in truth in place of the
Father. Originally a Father religion, Christianity became a Son religion. The fate of having to displace
the Father it could not escape.

Only a part of the Jewish people accepted the new doctrine. Those who refused to do so are still called Jews. Through this decision they are still more sharply separated from the rest of the world than they were before. They had to suffer the reproach from the new religious community—which besides Jews included Egyptians, Greeks, Syrians, Romans, and lastly also Teutons—that they had murdered God. In its full form this reproach would run: "They will not admit that they killed God, whereas we do and are cleansed from the guilt of it." Then it is easy to understand what truth lies behind this reproach. Why the Jews were unable to participate in the progress which this confession to the murder of God betokened (in spite of all its distortion) might well be the subject of a special investigation. Through this they have, so to speak, shouldered a tragic guilt. They have been made to suffer severely for it.

Our research has perhaps thrown some light on the question how the Jewish people acquired the qualities that characterize it. The problem how they could survive until today as an entity has not proved so easy to solve. One cannot, however, reasonably demand or expect exhaustive answers of such enigmas. All that I can offer is a simple contribution, and one which should be appraised with due regard to the critical limitations I have already mentioned.

Glossary

Ætiology: causation, particularly of disease.

Affect: pertaining to the feeling bases of emotion.

Ambivalence: the coexistence of opposed feelings, particularly love and hate

Amnesia: failure of memory

Cathexis: the process whereby ideas and mental attitudes are invested with a "charge" of emotion.

Imago: a German periodical devoted to the non-medical application of psychoanalysis.

Instinctual: pertaining to instinct.

Masochism: the obtaining of sexual pleasure in conjunction with suffering.

Obsessional neurosis: a neurosis characterized by the alternation of obsessive (compulsive) ideas and doubts.

Onanism: auto-erotic activity, the commonest example being masturbation.

Phylogenetic: pertaining to racial development.

Reaction-formation: development of a character trait that keeps in check and conceals another one, usually of the exactly opposite kind.

Regression: reversion to an earlier kind of mental life.

Repetition-compulsion: the tendency to repeat, which Freud considers the most fundamental characteristic of the mind.

Repression: the keeping of unacceptable ideas from consciousness—i.e., in the "unconscious."

Sadism: the obtaining of sexual pleasure through the infliction of suffering.

Super-Ego: the self-criticizing part of the mind out of which the conscience develops.

Trauma: injury, bodily or mental.

Index

SIGMUND FREUD, the founder of psychoanalysis, was born in Freiberg, Moravia, in 1856. He was educated in Vienna and received his degree of Doctor of Medicine at the University of Vienna in 1881. In 1885, already intensely interested in psychiatry, he went to Paris to study in the school of Charcot and Janet, the founders of modern abnormal psychology. There he began to develop his own method for investigating neurotic disorders by analysis. When he returned to Vienna in 1886 he began to practice psychoanalysis, and in 1902 he was made Professor Extraordinary of Neurology at the University of Vienna, an appointment he held until 1938, when the German occupation of Austria forced him to take refuge in England. He died there in 1939. MOSES AND MONOTHEISM was completed in London, and published in America by Alfred A. Knopf, Inc., in 1939.